PRAISE FOR FERNANDO ORS AND
SMARTER ALTERNATIVE INVESTMENTS

I've been working with Fernando for over seventeen years. He is a unique person, perhaps because of his philosophy of life formed in the dojo and his deep understanding of modern technologies and alternative investments.

When he presented his ideas to the board of directors or top executives of various companies, there were usually three phases of understanding them: hearing and not listening, listening and not understanding, and understanding and making them the property of the board members or top executives.

Fernando is a visionary, and time has proven him right so many times. Several years ago, I also specialized in blockchain, tokenization, and their legal regulations. Fernando and I coincided with this too, which is fascinating and challenging.

Reading this book has confirmed my view of him, whose friendship I am proud of, despite the distance that separates us from Spain to the United States.

I will recommend the book to friends and family members because it provides a wonderful framework for introspection,

identifying our priorities, and making genuine improvements to our lives. They will also extract very useful advice
on developing meaningful relationships, gaining leadership
skills, building wealth through ethically and fairly-minded
businesses, and, of course, on new technologies and alternative investments.

—**Jose Ramón Romero**
Partner
Loyra Lawyers

Smarter Alternative Investments is not only a faithful reflection
of how Fernando approaches his personal and professional life,
but it is also a life lesson. I can see Fernando in almost all of the
situations and advice described in this "must-read" book. It is
very comprehensive and easy to apply to our daily lives. Thank
you, Fernando, for sharing your "secret sauce" with us all.

—**Antonio López**
SVP
City National Bank

We spend our entire lives accumulating knowledge to become
better professionals. Universities and business schools teach us
the fundamentals of our disciplines: management, marketing,
finance, and more. However, building a successful professional
(and personal) career is impossible without some essential
lessons that only someone with rich and extensive experience
can share. That's why this book is a significant event.

—**Gonzalo Brujó**
Global CEO
Interbrand

Like good films based on true events, Fernando is able to transmit decades of learning—both at the personal and professional level—through this book. What's especially interesting is the "touch" he gives it by blending funny situations with profound business, personal, and even spiritual reflections. Undoubtedly, Fernando's book will help many find their way. One hundred percent recommended.

—Miguel Caballero
CEO
Tutellus

In this book, you will find hundreds of useful and insightful ideas from one of the smartest friends I am lucky to have. Pearls of wisdom and thoughts are shared from his experience and innermost being. It is a comprehensive approach that addresses both personal and financial matters. I strongly advise anyone interested in growing to read it.

—Luis Merino
Head of Balanced Funds
Santalucía Asset Management

I am honored to recommend Fernando's book. In its pages, you will find an inspiring vision of how we can transform our relationship with life, money, and investing. His innovative approach and passion for financial sustainability are contagious. Although our professional relationship is still in its infancy, I can say with confidence that his commitment to excellence and work ethic are admirable, and his ability to simplify complex concepts and make them accessible to all is a real strength. In short, this book is a must-read for anyone looking for an alternative perspective. You will learn something new and useful about investing, new technologies, and, more importantly, about how to impact your life and the world positively.

—Francisco Mariscal
CEO
Orbyn

This book, written with generosity and dedication by Fernando, is a powerful tool for transforming lives. Not only does he provide enlightening advice on business and investments, but he also inspires us to better our human relationships through purpose-sharing. It is a legacy of wisdom that will benefit each reader and make a difference in the world. I admire Fernando for his genuine commitment to helping as many people as possible and for his proficiency in expressing it.

—Eric Sánchez
CEO
Reental

Throughout elementary school, I was Fernando's closest friend. He was a charming and charismatic boy that most kids admired. We complimented one another so well that I remember feeling blessed to be so close to him. Fernando was aware of his strengths and weaknesses and always worked hard to get the best out of both, so I always knew he would be a successful man. Now, forty years later, I loved reading his book, which offers sage advice in a humble and straight-forward way, just like he always was!

—Javier Rodríguez Soler
Global Head of Corporate and Investment Banking
BBVA

I have known Fernando for a long time, both personally and professionally, and I have seen how he has always chosen the path of nonconformity, the path of "one step further."

He always grows, shares, adds value to everything we do, and strives for a positive footprint. Life and business are not incompatible; they are complementary, with common secrets and practical tools essential to master to leave a legacy. Reading his book inspires the pursuit of these objectives through the lens of a stimulating and infrequent global perspective. For this reason, I highly recommend it. It contains far more than you might think.

—**Hernán San Pedro López de Uribe**
Director
Investor Relations at SOCIMI LAR

This book will become a treasured companion on my nightstand. I will reread it again to internalize daily doses of wisdom that resonate deeply with my life's philosophy, and I will enjoy sharing it with my two young daughters. Each page encourages personal and economic growth and inspires us to extend our influence beyond our immediate circle. It's also a doorway to enter the passionate alternative investments world.

—**Carla Castelló**
COO
Reental

Smarter Alternative Investments is not a typical investment book. It is written in such a way that you will actually enjoy reading it. Whether you're just starting out or a seasoned professional, you will find key tips and mnemonics aids throughout the book. Chapter five, "A Path That Leads to Growth," is a masterpiece that you should always have printed out next to your desk.

—Nicolas Barilari
CEO
Nash21

Fernando's book brilliantly distills his approach to life and leadership—values that deeply influenced me during our time together. His belief in my abilities pushed me beyond my limits and taught me to embrace challenges and innovate fearlessly, just as he advises in his book. This book offers actionable wisdom for anyone navigating the complexities of personal and professional growth.

—Mariana Luciano
Head of Quality and Rankings
IE

Fernando's book offers a holistic approach to wealth, emphasizing not just financial gains but personal growth and lasting legacy. Through practical advice and personal anecdotes, Fernando guides readers through building meaningful relationships, enhancing leadership skills, and capitalizing on alternative investments to make a positive difference. This three-part journey into upgrading one's life, money, and legacy is both inspirational and practical, making sophisticated investment strategies accessible to everyone.

—Pablo Espuela
Mentor
MIT Innovation Fund

I have known Fernando for nearly thirty years. This book embodies his essence fully. It is a perfect synthesis of technology, innovation, leadership, and humanism. In a solid, rigorous, and friendly manner, he offers us his authentic life legacy.

—Alex Mahave
CEO
Be Your Best

Smarter Alternative Investments uses the heartwarming gift of life's teachings notes in a jar to provide readers with essential tools to enhance their social relationships and investments, adapt to the digital age, and find a purpose in their lives. Fernando candidly shares his experiences and insights as a successful entrepreneur. I'm lucky to have known him since our childhood; every interaction with him has been a learning experience for me.

—Juan Pablo Soriano
Managing Director
Top US Rating Agency

I would like to convey my heartfelt appreciation for Fernando's generous gift to us, his daughters, and the rest of humanity. We all need this insightful book filled with experiences and advice with excellent literary quality and essential technical knowledge. It's a delight to read it in a passionate, existential tone. I am really proud of my friend Fernando.

This book enhances people's quality of life and bridges the gap between traditional methods and the greatest current technological innovations. We gain knowledge and develop into more cultivated individuals with each refined quote and experience that is shared. It enables us to evaluate our personal and professional lives in order to lead better new ones. I especially enjoyed the chapters about the potential of alternative investments, particularly when he discusses art and uses our company Fidelitas ARTe as an example of how we are optimizing and democratizing art investing by combining art, finance, and technology.

—Ruben Pugna
Founder, President
Fidelitas ARTe

Meeting Fernando and reading his book, *Smarter Alternative Investments: Upgrade Your Money and Your Life*, were memorable experiences. Our conversations seem to have come to life in these pages. Fernando has always been able to make the complicated simple and put his heart into what he does. Reading his book, I felt like I was with him, picking up his usual useful tips and optimism. This book gave me pointers on how to be smarter with investments and inspired me to be a better person by reminding me of the importance of acting with values and kindness. It is a reflection of how Fernando approaches life and now encourages all of us to improve ours.

—Richard Gracia
CEO
Thrive Colivings
Best-Selling Author

Fernando Ors, an entrepreneur, innovator, and eternal optimist from a family of communicators, shares his life philosophy, business thoughts, and investing strategies with us, along with some of his favorite quotes and noteworthy events. I suggest reading it in small doses to both enjoy and better assimilate the author's wise messages and noble intentions.

—Jose Antonio Martinez Sampedro
Founder
Codere

Smarter Alternative Investments: Upgrade Your Money and Your Life helps you understand investing as a smart and purposeful way to leave a lasting legacy, a key element for your future and future generations. I love how Fernando addresses the importance of this perspective.

—Gustavo Rossi
Founder
Alquiler Seguro

Smarter Alternative Investments: Upgrade Your Money and Your Life is a life advice compendium where Fernando Ors reveals deeply personal anecdotes and the lessons he has learned from many years of experience living and working in various organizations around the world. Fernando presents his views on maximizing investment strategies through alternative investments that have become more accessible thanks to the advent of the latest technologies, such as blockchain and tokenization. A lovely gift for his daughters, friends, and anyone who wishes to live a more abundant and meaningful life while diversifying on smarter alternative investments.

—Montse Garrido
Latin America Public Sector Head
Citibank

"No one alone" is the essential principle of Fernando's life philosophy that I admire. Many people are figuring out how to build the life they want. You could be one of them. If you want financial progress and a prosperous life, don't be frightened of investing; instead, be terrified not to invest. This book outlines the fundamentals for starting your journey.

—**Andrea Redondo**
Founder
"El Club de Inversión"
Financially free before turning thirty

This is an essential guide for those looking to enrich their personal and financial lives. Divided into three parts—Upgrade Your Life, Your Money, and Your Legacy—this book offers a unique blend of practical advice and investment philosophy, emphasizing the accessibility of alternative investments thanks to modern technology. Fernando teaches readers how to develop meaningful relationships and leadership skills and guides them through building wealth through businesses and investments that positively impact the world, emphasizing the importance of kindness in all endeavors. Ideal for both entrepreneurs and seasoned investors, this book is a must-read for anyone who wants to leave a lasting legacy.

—**Patricia Pastor**
GP
Next Tier Ventures

This book is an entertaining compendium of the author's financial and emerging technologies knowledge. It also contains practical advice for personal and professional growth from the author's firsthand experiences. Everyone, especially the younger generation, needs this easy-to-consult legacy.

—**María Bujidos**
Director
Codere

Fernando Ors is one of those people who, without losing humility, nourish you and add value from the first moment. *Smarter Alternative Investments: Upgrade Your Money and Your Life* invites you to think outside the box and definitely expands your vision and capacity for action. It gives you the key tools to achieve your best version.

—**Florencia Minadeo**
Cofounder
LinkUp

Smarter Alternative Investments: Upgrade Your Money and Your Life speaks to current and future generations, offering sage advice on life, business, and how everyone can access alternative investments thanks to today's technology. Throughout the three-part book, Ors shows readers how to develop meaningful relationships, gain leadership skills, and build wealth through businesses and investments that make a positive impact by being, first and foremost, kind.

—**Eduardo Morales**
Business Advisor
Ficom Leisure

This is a great legacy.

—Sebastien Dupoy
Head of the Caribbean Region
FreeBalance

I read it, and it is marvelous.

—Nick Papadoglou
Board Member
Nexi

In this exciting new era of groundbreaking technology, Fernando provides guidance on how to approach it and diversify our portfolios to boost our returns through alternative investments.

—Carlos Blanco
Chairman
Encomenda Capital

Fernando's wisdom reminds us of the transience of life and the importance of seizing every moment. His book inspires us to expect little from others and to serve with love, pardoning those who lack comprehension. He guides us toward wholeness, encouraging us to find our purpose and create a beneficial influence on others. His advice on wellness, leadership, and alternative investing illuminates the route to achievement and personal fulfillment—an unparalleled book that will transcend generations!

—Pedro Ramón López Garcia
CEO
Climatecoin

I recently came across Fernando, and he left quite an impression on me. His insights into life, investing, and pursuing something greater than mere profit are truly enlightening. He's passionate about sharing his experiences and wisdom, with a sincere desire to mentor the young and not-so-young alike. This book is a must-read, appealing to those with youthful spirits and anyone seeking to enrich their journey through life.

—Enrique López de Ceballos
Partner
Protein Capital

Throughout my life, I have always wished that I had learned all I could about wealth early on: how to create it, invest it, and preserve it. Unfortunately, we do not learn this until we are confronted with the realities of working life. This book offers just that: a "wealth framework," a set of guiding principles that encompasses everything Fernando has learned over the course of his extensive and multifaceted life and career. He has now distilled all his knowledge and guidance into a book he can share with people like me who may not be very familiar with the business and investment world. Fernando has done a fantastic job of synthesizing what really matters in building wealth and the key characteristics a person should have for a fulfilled life. For any person, whether young and looking for guidance on how to start building their wealth early or older and looking to consolidate their general investment knowledge, this book is a must and an entertaining read.

—Carlos de la Morena
Ambassador of Spain to El Salvador

"*Smarter Alternative Investments* is a testament to Fernando's unique approach to life and work, encapsulating the wisdom he has accumulated since we studied together for our MBA at IESE. This book is a great collection of experiences and strategies, and reflects Fernando's life, business, and investment philosophy. His insights, presented with clarity and humor, offer invaluable guidance for navigating personal growth and financial acumen. I strongly encourage anyone committed to personal and professional development to delve into this invaluable resource."

—Emilio Gayo
CEO
Telefónica Spain

"In three detailed sections—Upgrading Your Life, Your Money, and Your Legacy—Fernando invites us on a transformative journey that begins with cultivating deep, meaningful relationships, moves through mastering alternative investments leveraging modern technologies such as tokenization or decentralized finance (DeFi), and culminates in how creating a positive, tangible legacy. By sharing personal development wisdom, keen investment insights that open up new wealth-creation opportunities for everyone, and immersing us in the power of purposeful living to create a lasting impact legacy, Fernando empowers us to upgrade our lives improving the lives of others."

—Ismael Cala
Former CNN & Univision Host,
Life Strategist and Bestselling Author

SMARTER
ALTERNATIVE
INVESTMENTS

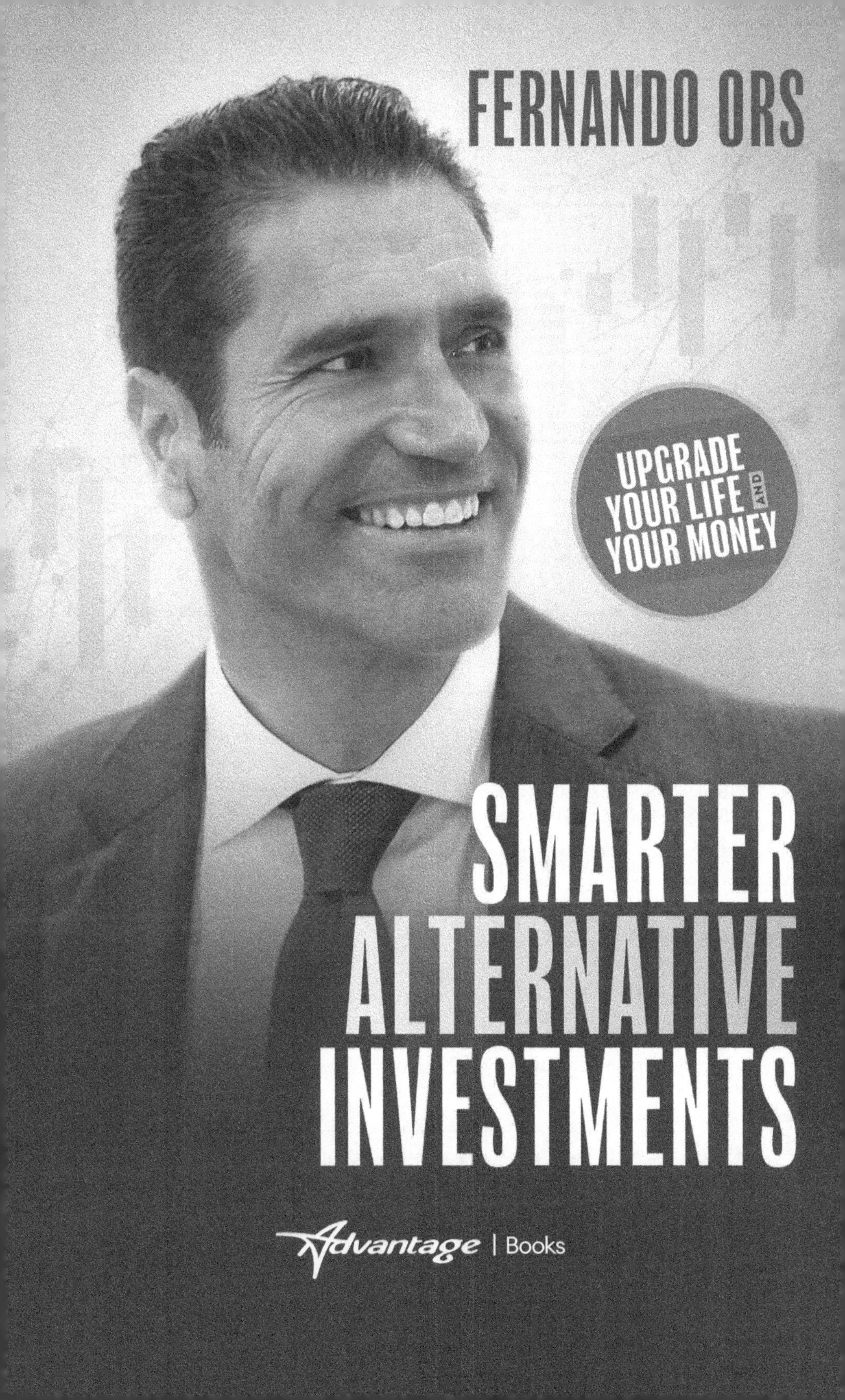

FERNANDO ORS

UPGRADE
YOUR LIFE AND
YOUR MONEY

SMARTER
ALTERNATIVE
INVESTMENTS

Advantage | Books

Copyright © 2024 by Fernando Ors.

All rights reserved. No part of this book may be used or reproduced in any manner whatsoever without prior written consent of the author, except as provided by the United States of America copyright law.

Published by Advantage Books, Charleston, South Carolina.
An imprint of Advantage Media.

ADVANTAGE is a registered trademark, and the Advantage colophon is a trademark of Advantage Media Group, Inc.

Printed in the United States of America.

10 9 8 7 6 5 4 3 2 1

ISBN: 979-8-89188-050-4 (Paperback)
ISBN: 979-8-89188-051-1 (eBook)

Library of Congress Control Number: 2024910589

Cover design by Lance Buckley.
Layout design by Matthew Morse.

This publication is designed to provide accurate and authoritative information in regard to the subject matter covered. It is sold with the understanding that the publisher is not engaged in rendering legal, accounting, or other professional services. If legal advice or other expert assistance is required, the services of a competent professional person should be sought.

Advantage Books is an imprint of Advantage Media Group. Advantage Media helps busy entrepreneurs, CEOs, and leaders write and publish a book to grow their business and become the authority in their field. Advantage authors comprise an exclusive community of industry professionals, idea-makers, and thought leaders. For more information go to **advantagemedia.com**.

To my daughters, nieces, and nephews.

I once heard a woman on the radio say,
"If I had known forty years ago what I know now …"
and I always wondered what she was referring to.

As the years went by, I understood that she was
probably not referring to a specific piece of knowledge
but to a sum of life experiences.

Well, forty years later, here is my particular answer ;)

CONTENTS

PART 2
UPGRADE YOUR MONEY

PART 3
UPGRADE YOUR LEGACY

INTRODUCTION

Gather my extended family together, and you're bound to hear lively discussions. Meals together often include debates that span a wide range of topics. We might talk about politics, business ideas, economics, alternative investments, and life in general—all in a short time.

Of all the family discussions that I've had, one will forever remain in my mind. In fact, it is what motivated me to write this book. It happened years ago now. My two daughters were young then. My father, a famous TV journalist, was still with us. But when I close my eyes, I can still see it play out like it was today.

This memory occurred during a summer family lunch. While I don't necessarily remember the topic being discussed, I do remember that I was there with my father and other relatives. A debate about something—maybe macroeconomics or a global war event—escalated into an argument and eventually hit a climax. I made a statement, and my father retorted, "I do not agree, and you have never taught me anything." That was the end of the discussion.

The comment from my father hurt me deeply. At the time, I didn't believe my father truly grasped the level of pain his words had inflicted on me. We never spoke of it again.

One day, after my father's passing, that memory surfaced, and I felt the sting all over again. Soon I found myself secluded within the confines of my room, absorbed in tears.

My immediate family at that time, which included my wife and two young and innocent daughters, discovered my distress. They learned about the sorrow I bore because of the argument that arose during that family lunch.

Some weeks later, my daughters surprised me with a gift. They had been moved by learning about how much my father's words had hurt me. In response, they had filled a glass jar with delicate scraps of paper. Each piece contained a quote about personal growth, business, or investments I had shared with them throughout their lives. The jar bore a label adorned with the words, "Dad Life Lessons." The title was encircled by their heartfelt drawings, expressions of their love.

When I received the gift, I knew that most of the quotes would be short. I have always tried to synthesize relevant learning in a few words due to my dyslexia, because it makes it easier to create as well as recall.

During the years that followed, I made sure the jar was always in our household. This took some effort, as we regularly move. We changed locations nineteen times during the last twenty-five years, going to places all over the world. We have lived or spent extended time in countries such as Singapore, Indonesia, Italy, and in several states of the United States such as California, Georgia, and Florida. Everywhere we went, that jar went with us.

As time went on, I resolved to preserve those cherished quotes. I wanted to transcribe them onto pages that would last. I also wanted these quotes to be readily accessible, recognizing that half a century of existence grants one a measure of maturity to impart to others.

And yet, there's more to this story. As I gathered the scraps of paper and began adding more lessons to them that I had accumulated, since my daughters created the jar of quotes, I had a realization. We are living in an increasingly digital world. The trend allows for new ways to communicate. It provides more opportunities to share and learn from each other.

Given this, I recognized the chance to develop material that could be accessed by my daughters now, as I write this as a gift for their dual degree graduation, and in the future. Moreover, others could tap into the lessons as they navigate their own paths. The guidance and advice could serve as my own avatar. Think of an assistant that can be tapped for answers. When you do so, you can gain the information you need to make smart choices.

That's the goal of this book. By reading it, you'll learn about how you can invest in a smarter way both in your personal and financial life. You'll take away timeless tools that you can use to improve your relationships and your investments and to live a purposeful life. You'll also spot trends and technologies that are disrupting many industries. Once you know and analyze them in-depth, you will discover new smarter alternative ways to invest and live.

I've spent my career working in innovative areas and tech companies that I am passionate about, since they allowed me to help and positively impact industries and people. As a serial intrapreneur and entrepreneur, I've been involved in start-ups, and led multinational digital transformations, always with a goal of making a transgenerational social impact, adding more than twenty years of experience in strategic consulting, international business development, and value and alternative investing.

When joining companies, I've always evaluated their key performance indicators (KPIs), in the sense of their "key positive impacts'" rather than "key performance indicators." This is important to me, as I want to help make a difference, and I found many ways to do that.

During my time at Codere and Intralot, for example, I mentored employees and led the way to regulations that dedicate gaming taxes to educational scholarships. When I launched BrightStar, it was with the mission of avoiding or minimizing the risk that no one would have to leave this world, like my father, alone in a cold hospital bed, due to the COVID protocol; under the motto "no one alone," individuals should be assisted in their transition to the other world accompanied by ideally a loved one. At Reental and Fidelitas ARTe, my passion to make real estate and art investing accessible to everyone is a driver and motivation to work hard every day. Through Savia Group, which includes Savia Consulting, Savia Health, and Savia Capital, I assist with the international expansion of companies, the development of healthtech businesses, and the education and portfolio management around alternative investments.

And my journey continues. I've lived, with my beloved wife, in more than ten countries across Asia, Europe, and America, and managed teams of more than twenty nationalities. I see life as a continual learning process. What we do today makes a difference for our loved ones and for those who live tomorrow.

By reading this book, you can get a glimpse of what I've learned along the way. Moreover, you'll receive food for thought as I share some peculiar habits or skills that you can consider to apply in your path of growth. The chapters provide tips to upgrade both your life and your money.

You'll learn about the importance of relationships and how to have an open mindset. You'll also discover the power of a personal circle, and how having a sense of purpose can be life changing. You'll gather insight on how to make the most of your growth and opportunities, along with communication and leadership traits. You'll see how managing your health, self-esteem, and a balanced life can make you go farther than expected and enjoy the path.

You'll also find out that there are new and smarter alternatives to improve your finances, including methods that branch away from traditional models. Some of them aren't well-known and used yet, but they will be more prominent in the near future. Thanks to new technologies, protocols, and platforms, you can invest more efficiently and on your own terms. You can make short- or long-term commitments and withdraw funds when you need them. These latest trends are allowing many more people to access opportunities that weren't available to them before.

In the following pages, you will see some of the quotes I initially shared with my daughters. Once presented to me in a jar will be presented to the entire world. My hope is that they will help us build and grow together so that when we think of each other, it will be in a positive, productive way.

I still have conversations with my extended family, and they often turn into debates. Yet, over the years, I've leaned into using humor to help us cope with difficult discussions and life in general. Following this life philosophy, I've sprinkled touches of fun at the beginning of each chapter. They reflect one of my favorite approaches to life and work, which is, whatever happens, keep smiling.

You can start from the beginning and read to the end—or jump in whatever chapter you are more interested in. However you prefer, I hope you enjoy it!

PART 1

UPGRADE YOUR LIFE

© Glasbergen/ glasbergen.com

"You changed your Facebook relationship status
347 times today. Want to talk about it?"

CHAPTER 1

IT STARTS WITH RELATIONSHIPS

One day in my youth I came home late. It was nearly dawn. Full disclosure: I had been out and returned after a bender. At the time, we were having summer holidays in Aguilas, a small village of Murcia, Spain, where we have a beachfront house in front of the Isla del Fraile (Monk Island).

As I approached our home, I quickly realized I wasn't alone. There was my mother, standing in the doorway. She was waiting for me. She had probably been there for a long time since I had been out all night.

Instinctively, I knew there would be a quarrel. My mother would be concerned about my safety and likely didn't approve of my arrival time.

Sure enough, a run-in followed. But then, as we calmed down, I looked around and took in our surroundings. The sun was about to rise just behind the island. Spurred on by the beauty of the moment,

I invited my mother to join me on the terrace to watch the sun come up.

She agreed. I took advantage of those next minutes together to pour out my soul to her. I told her how grateful I was for her efforts and sacrifices to raise my siblings and myself. I expressed thankfulness for her principles, values, and habits that she had taught us. From her, we learned everything from having an interest in reading and movies to showing unconditional love to others despite their flaws.

I don't remember how long we talked. I do, however, recall that after the sun rose, we went back into the house and parted ways. Before I went to bed, she found me. She was crying and gave me the longest hug I had ever been given.

The next day, my father found me. "I don't know what you said to your mother yesterday, but thank you," he said. "She says she has never felt so happy."

Even today, I have memories of that sunrise and explosion of emotions. Ever since that moment, I have been committed to living near water. On an island, by the sea, as I currently live, I find I am the calmest—and remember what's important in life.

Regardless of the point of life you're in, relationships matter. They are well worth the investment, and you'll learn from others. You can laugh together, cry together, go through experiences together, and grow together. I always like to approach people by remembering to ask, "How would you treat that person if it were the last time you were going to talk to them because you were going to die tomorrow by accident or natural death?" It helps me keep perspective and to treat everyone with kindness.

In the following sections, I share some quotes and lessons on relationships and friendships. Many of these I have gleaned from mentors and books, and then added my own twist to them. I hope they inspire you to reflect on your own relationships. As you read through them, or come back to them later, I encourage you to think about what you can do, today, to connect more or better with people you care about.

ON RELATIONSHIPS

MAKE IT AN INFINITE POSITIVE SUM GAME

Make others love to meet or play nonstop with you. Avoid tit for tats. Look for win-wins since nobody wins until we all do. Prioritize being in a relationship over being right because you can't always have both.

BE OPEN TO THE GOOD YOU CAN FIND

Loving means focusing on the best in each other, even if you have seen the worst. Remember that different perspectives can be eye-opening, so be attentive to the remarks of your friends and colleagues.

TAKE YOUR TIME TO NURTURE YOUR RELATIONSHIPS

The cliché seems to be true: According to some studies, couples that spend more fun time together stay together longer.[1] Oxytocin, the love-sex hormone, is released when partners engage in mutually satisfying activities. Create time for your partner, no matter how busy life gets. Take a break when needed and take it easy on the people around you when they need it.

ACTIONS MATTER MORE THAN WORDS

You might say or feel many things, but you only transform this world whenever you add smart or kind action to those words or feelings.

---

1   "Couples That Play Together Stay Together," BYU, https://foreverfamilies.byu.edu/couples-that-play-together-stay-together#:~:text=So%20far%2C%20the%20findings%20are,spouse%20can%20improve%20your%20marriage.

That's exactly why they say actions speak louder than words. Speaking of "speaking louder," it is also said that speaking in a loud voice is one of the characteristics of a confident person. *So, in doubt, no matter how weak your points or jokes are, crack them LOUDLY.*

LOVING IS LIKE THE WEATHER WITH ITS SUNSHINE, STORMS, SNOWFLAKES, AND HAIL

Be ready to encounter moments of difficulty and turmoil with your loved ones. It may be conflicts, disagreements, or even heartache. However, you will weather the storms and embrace the beauty of life's snowflakes since each of us carries a unique story.

YOU CANNOT PADDLE YOUR BOAT ALONE[2]

Make as many friends as possible. Remember that your happiness and success depend, most of the time, on others. As the athlete Diana Nyad, who at the age of sixty embarked on a nearly impossible lifelong dream of swimming from Cuba to Florida across more than one hundred miles of open ocean, said when she achieved it after several trials and more than sixty hours of nonstop swimming, "Never, ever give up. You're never too old to chase your dreams, and it takes a team!"

LOOK AT THEIR PARENTS IF YOU WANT TO KNOW WHAT YOUR PARTNER WILL PROBABLY LOOK LIKE IN THE FUTURE

This applies to both physical and psychological aspects. Look how their parents relate to each other, their hobbies, professions, entrepre-

---

2   William McRaven, "William McRaven Quotes,"
     Goodreads.com, https://www.goodreads.com/
     quotes/8940622-you-cannot-paddle-the-boat-alone-find-someone-to-share.

neurship spirit, etc. This will give you some input about their probable future behavior and interests.

BE A DETAIL FREAK

If you are careless in small matters, you will not be trusted with important matters.

SETTLE ARGUMENTS QUICKLY

Never end the day without apologizing to those who deserve it.

HANG OUT WITH THE RIGHT PEOPLE

We mirror those around us. We become the average of the five people we spend the most time with, so be selective about who you surround yourself with. Don't be with folks who hold you back. They should be positive, self-controlled people pushing you up. Look at your circle and choose your friends and partners wisely!

MAKE SMART USE OF SOCIAL MEDIA

Make good use of social networks and digital technology to cultivate meaningful relationships or to make your services or businesses more appealing. Make sure that their algorithms do not manipulate you by hijacking your most valuable asset, which is your time.

BE CREATIVE WITH FAMILY OUTING PLANS

Find common hobbies, sports, movies, restaurants, and trips that fit everybody's tastes. Transform them into the best birthday or Christmas presents.

DON'T ASK, "HOW WAS YOUR DAY?" INSTEAD SAY, "TELL ME ABOUT YOUR DAY"

You will avoid monosyllables and short answers.

THE LESS YOU HAVE TO LIFT, THE HIGHER YOU CAN RISE

Get rid of unneeded baggage, clothes you don't really like, and people that complicate your life. Begin with those who gossip, as they waste a lot of your time. Additionally, as the Spanish proverb says, "Whoever gossips will gossip about you."

GIVE WITHOUT EXPECTING; RECEIVE WITHOUT FORGETTING

And never forget who was with you when no one else was. Share with others, and they'll surprise you in return with their own favors.

LEND MONEY IF YOU CAN, BUT NOT TWICE IN A ROW WITHOUT REPAYMENT OF THE FIRST AMOUNT

Throughout your life, you will have partners, friends, and relatives who will ask you to borrow money for different unforeseen events and hardships. Nothing is more pleasant than being able to help your family and friends when they need it, but if someone does not pay you back the initial amount borrowed, *sorry, but game over.*

MONEY IS A DEAD TREASURE—CHILDREN A LIVING ONE

Always consider your children's opinions as members of your team (and family is your most relevant team). Remember that there is no place for punishment in a caring relationship.

Punishment may stop bad behavior, but it can also prevent children from learning to correct themselves, so teach them to learn from their mistakes and give them opportunities to improve things on their own.

LOVE IS NOT A FEELING; IT IS AN ATTITUDE

The more you judge, the less you love. Feed your relationships by prioritizing having fun together as opposed to menial tasks. Take some photos together as a reminder of your common journey toward a happier and healthier life together.

WHEN EVERYTHING IS SAID AND DONE, ONLY LOVE WILL LAST

After all is said and done, there is a lot more said than done. Identify the ten most important people in your life and focus on loving them.

WRITE A LOVE MESSAGE TO YOUR PARTNER TODAY

Example: "I loved it when you helped me pack my suitcase on my way to the airport today." And since you are already writing, take the opportunity to write down, just for you, what you like about your partner, and never let their weaknesses overwhelm you.

WHEN A CHILD ASKS FOR HELP, GIVE IT; WHEN A CHILD ASKS YOU TO PLAY, PLAY

When a child asks a question, answer it. When a child asks to do something fun, do it. Avoid the typical excuses, such as "I am busy," "In a minute," or "After this call." The point is, one day, they will never ask.

A PROBLEM SHARED IS HALF SOLVED

A problem not addressed will remain unsolved. But a problem shared is half solved. Ask your partner, coach, or mentor when the best time is to talk.

FIND THE RIGHT MENTORS

Seneca, on the brevity of life, stated, "We are in the habit of saying that it was not in our power to choose the parents who were allotted to us, that they were given to us by chance. But we can choose whose children we would like to be."[3]

EXPRESS SINCERE PRAISES OR GRATITUDE AS MUCH AS YOU CAN

In a survey of two thousand Americans, it was found that most people believed that expressing gratitude to a coworker makes them feel happier and more fulfilled. Yet the same survey found that on any given day, only 10 percent of employees express gratitude to someone at work.[4] As always, try to be in the top 10 percent.

---

3 Seneca, "Seneca Quotes," Goodreads.com, https://www.goodreads.com/ quotes/8945853-we-are-in-the-habit-of-saying-that-it-was.

4 "Expressing Gratitude May Be True Key to Happiness, Survey Finds," StudyFinds. com, September 15, 2022, https://studyfinds.org/gratitude-key-to-happiness/.

FRIENDSHIP

GOOD FRIENDS ARE LIKE STARS. YOU DON'T ALWAYS SEE THEM, BUT YOU KNOW THEY'RE ALWAYS THERE (CHRISTY EVANS)[5]

During difficult moments when life feels ugly and awful, friends become a beacon of light. Through shared experiences and memories, they become an integral part of our story, shaping who we are. And according to some studies the emotional support provided positively impacts our immune system and longevity![6]

EVEN FROM A DISTANCE, YOU CAN ENJOY THE WARMTH OF YOUR FRIENDSHIP

Long-distance friendships offer a unique opportunity for exploration and discovery. Through our friends' eyes, we gain insights into different lifestyles and perspectives. We learn about new places, experiences, and ways of thinking that broaden our horizons and deepen our understanding of the world.

LOVE AND FRIENDSHIP ARE NOT ASKED FOR LIKE WATER; THEY ARE OFFERED LIKE TEA

And at the same time, if you want to win a friend, don't do him a favor; ask him to do it for you.

---

5   Christy Evans, "Christy Evans Quotes," Goodreads.com, https://www.goodreads.com/quotes/7926961-good-friends-are-like-stars-you-don-t-always-see-them.

6   Maija Reblin and Bert N. Uchino, "Social and Emotional Support and Its Implication for Health," *Current Opinion in Psychiatry* 21, no. 2 (2009): 201–205, https://www.ncbi.nlm.nih.gov/pmc/articles/PMC2729718/.

WHEN TALKING BECOMES MORE IMPORTANT THAN LISTENING, IT IS PREFERABLE TO CHANGE FRIENDS

Find friends that are interested in what you have to say, and then listen to them. As they speak, focus on their words instead of building an argument. Slow down the pace of the conversation to help the other person feel heard. Always smile, as smiling always helps to relieve everyone's tension.

BE FUN TO BE AROUND

If you spend your time chasing butterflies, they'll fly away. But if you spend your time making a beautiful garden, the butterflies will come. Don't chase; attract.

LOOK TO LEARN FROM OTHERS

As Carl Gustav Jung stated, "If a man knows more than others, he becomes lonely."[7]

AVOID THE FRENEMIES OUTSIDE OF SOCIAL EVENTS

We've all been a frenemy at one point or another. We've been nice to someone's face because there was something in it for us, but we did not feel well in their company. With so many social events, this is going to be unavoidable—however, try to avoid false friendship at all costs. If you are good, straightforward, and well-meaning, it should show in your eyes and not escape notice.

---

7   Carl Gustav Jung, "Carl Gustav Jung Quotes," Goodreads.com, https://www. goodreads.com/quotes/tag/carl-gustav-jung.

TO REACH YOUR GOALS, YOU WILL NEED ASSISTANCE FROM YOUR FRIENDS, FAMILY, AND ASSOCIATES

The best way to encourage them to help you is to offer to help them first. Build trust, establish a sense of camaraderie, create a positive ripple effect, and foster an environment where everyone is motivated to contribute to one another's success. The path to achieving our goals is interwoven with the collective efforts of a supportive network. As the Godfather said, "Keep your friends close and your enemies closer."

IF YOU FORGET EVERYTHING ELSE, REMEMBER THIS

Express your appreciation. Tell someone what a difference he or she has made in your life. *Amor vincit omnia.*

Whenever I think of that dawn, sitting on the terrace with my mother, I remember all the sufferings that I put her through and all the principles and values that she taught me with her example. First and foremost, she showed me what it takes to be in a relationship in capital letters. Her level of commitment to her family and raising her five children was unsurpassed. She worked hard and passed on traits of character, love, and responsibility to me and my siblings.

And when I look into the ocean today, I am reminded of the many people that have entered my life and taught me valuable lessons. Some are with me only in memory, but they are forever imprinted on my heart. They have helped me become who I am today, and they have motivated me to look for ways to be a light to others.

"My wife says I need new underwear.
Find out if it's cheaper for me to buy or lease."

UPGRADE YOUR LIFE WITH A PERSONAL CIRCLE

Besides the critical aspect of developing from the inside to the outside as a person, I have found that forming strong relationships with others can help you go farther than you could on your own. There are different rings within a personal circle to consider. It often starts with a partner, then extends to close family and friends. Professionally, having strong professional connections at work will help you continually learn and grow in your career, too.

For me, my close circle begins with my wife. She is a principal friend in my life, as well as a mentor and business partner. We run several companies together, and she is especially brilliant with numbers, accounting, and taxes, which complements my skills. When I reflect on my own journey, I would say that much of my personal and professional development is due to her presence.

When you look for someone to share your life with, it's crucial to find a person you can trust 100 percent. If you are lucky, as I have been, to have a partner who will work alongside you and add their own strengths to the relationship, you'll be able to form a strong team. My wife has lived with me in all kinds of countries around the world, and at every location, she motivates me to give my best.

Next in the circle I always consider my family most important. As my two daughters have grown up, I find myself gathering lessons from them. They bring a new perspective for me to review. As a family, we appreciate the effort and sacrifice it takes to make an impact, and we also celebrate every step forward.

After a spouse and loved ones come the remaining personal and professional connections. I have had close friendships with individuals including my friends from my beloved "patio," my youth, college, masters, Aguilas and Key Biscayne (I'll leave out names because it's a long list, but my daughters and they know who they are). Having bonds with coworkers and others in your life can help you find support when you need it most. You may already have a close network of individuals who will listen and be there for you. They might offer advice and praise at the right times too. If you don't have many personal and professional connections, keep your eyes open and you could find them in the most unexpected places.

When you do that, the possibilities can be great. During my career, an anecdote that I remember with special fondness is when, through an introduction facilitated by my brother-in-law, I was able to meet the chairman and CEO of Codere. The company, which specialized in gaming, was getting ready for an IPO, and I was brought on to assist them with a digital transformation through initially a six-month consultation agreement. There I worked with an incredible team (they also know who they are). As I look back on my time with these colleagues, I realize I learned something from every one of them. Some taught me how to express constructive criticism, and others showed me ways to be positive. In the end, I stayed for almost twenty years. During that time, Codere grew from a family business to be a multinational gaming group with more than twenty thousand employees and yearly revenues of over $12 billion. And I was not only part of it, but I enjoyed its business development and international growth thanks to the results that came from me building a close personal circle.

Expanding beyond these relationships, I consider myself to have many mentors from the digital and print world. Thanks to books, podcasts, movies based on real events (my favorite ones), and other forms of media, I have greatly increased my knowledge and perspective on life. If you listen closely, you may find the message you need to solve a problem or move forward.

As you think about and choose your own circle, I encourage you to look for others who are thoughtful and wise. Stay close to those who have great insights and intuition. Reduce the number of individuals in your life who are toxic or don't assist you at this moment. While some of what happens to you could be based on luck, for the most part, the outcome depends on the choices made. If you're surrounded by individuals on the wrong path, such as drug addiction or other unhealthy habits, you could fall into the same trap. Instead, find others who share the following philosophies in life.

As you think about and choose your own circle, I encourage you to look for others who are thoughtful and wise. Stay close to those who have great insights and intuition.

WISDOM AND INTUITION

EACH SEASON HAS ITS BEAUTY

The year has four seasons. Your life—and some days—has seasons, too.

DON'T HURRY, DON'T WORRY

If you're in a rush, you'll lose out on the wonderful now.

ALL THINGS HAPPEN FOR A REASON

Most of the time we cannot grasp the "why." As powerless as we are over what happens to us in life, we have the ability to choose how we respond.

DO NOT TAKE IT PERSONALLY

Avoid feeding your ego and awaken your essence. The ego is defensive, the essence proactive.

LIFE'S PERIODS OF CALM BETWEEN HARDSHIPS MAKE IT BEAUTIFUL

Learn to appreciate the good periods because the painful ones arise, too.

BE GRATEFUL, ALWAYS

Give thanks every night for the things you have in your life. Don't take the basics for granted; many others don't have them.

LOOK TO WORK TOGETHER

When you have ideas you want to develop, ask and collaborate with others. New inputs can help you take your original vision to the next level.

THERE ARE ALWAYS SILVER LINES IN THE CLOUDS

And light at the end of the tunnel.

CHAPTER 2: UPGRADE YOUR LIFE WITH A PERSONAL CIRCLE

BEHIND THE DARKEST CLOUDS AND STORMS SHINES THE RADIANT SUN

Be patient and embrace the unexpected.

THERE IS NOTHING GOOD OR BAD, BUT THINKING MAKES IT SO (WILLIAM SHAKESPEARE)

The idea is that our interpretations are more important than the things we experience. What you think about your experiences is more important than the experiences themselves, so use your thinking well and, if necessary, change the way you think. After that, change the way you act. Elon Musk noted Walter Isaacson's quote, "As Shakespeare teaches us, all heroes have flaws, some tragic, some conquered, and those we cast as villains can be complex."[8]

IT IS NOT ABOUT THE DESTINATION BUT THE TRAJECTORY

We may never arrive at the desired destination. Still, we can enjoy the way, and enjoy the now.

YOUR ROOTS ARE YOUR PRINCIPLES AND VALUES

Choose them wisely since your fruits and flowers will depend on them.

---

8 Elon Musk and Walter Isaacson, "Walter Isaacson Quotes," Goodreads.com, https://www.goodreads.com/quotes/11907582-as-shakespeare-teaches-us-all-heroes-have-flaws-some-tragic.

DO WHAT MAKES YOU HAPPY

Be kind and avoid hurting others. Remember Thich Nhat Hanh's recommendation: "The future is being made out of the present, so the best way to take care of the future is to take care of the present moment."[9]

LIFE'S JOURNEY IS A MARATHON, NOT A SPRINT

Life is like a long hurdles race paved with ups and downs, unforeseen events, and constant learning. Know that after every storm there is always calm, so enjoy every stage of it!

CARPE DIEM

Seneca shared, "Let us therefore set out wholeheartedly, leaving aside our many distractions and exert ourselves in this single purpose, before we realize too late the swift and unstoppable flight of time and are left behind. As each day arises, welcome it as the very best day of all, and make it your own possession. We must seize what flees."[10]

READ A LOT

The person you will be in five years will depend on the people you meet and the books you read. All the broad-based education books not only pay for themselves many times over, but they will also expand

---

9   Thich Nhat Hanh, "Thich Nhat Quotes," Goodreads.com, accessed January 17, 2024, https://www.goodreads.com/quotes/8587718-the-future-is-being-made-out-of-the-present-so.

10   Dave Eisley, "The Discipline of Action," LinkedIn, October 27, 2017, https://www.linkedin.com/pulse/discipline-action-dave-eisley-/?trk=pulse-article_more-articles_related-content-card.

your mind and knowledge. Warren Buffett attributes his success to just reading and thinking.[11] Emulate his example.

PURSUE A LIFE OF LEARNING

Educate yourself constantly and seek out wisdom from previous generations. Adding new skills and experiences will make you more valuable. Remember that the purpose of education is not knowledge but action, and that the best way to learn something is to teach it.

THE BIGGER THE STRUGGLE, THE BIGGER THE OPPORTUNITY

The greater the risk, the greater the gain. The greater the cost, the greater the benefit. Make the most of every challenge and difficulty, because the more uncomfortable you are, the more you will learn. Life is like a roulette table where you are given a limited number of chips, and once you place a chip, you can't get it back. In fact, you never walk away with chips in hand, so choose your bets and spend those chips wisely.

IN DOUBT, FOLLOW YOUR HEART AND INTUITION

If you cannot make use of objective data or advice, meet the silence, and listen to your essence. For the Arabs, silence is the wall of wisdom.

---

11   Marcel Schwantes, "Warren Buffett: What Separates Successful People from the Pack Really Comes Down to 1 Mental Habit," Inc.com, January 6, 2024, https://www.inc.com/marcel-schwantes/warren-buffett-what-separates-successful-people-from-pack-really-comes-down-to-1-mental-habit.html.

LEARN SILENCE FROM THE CHATTERBOXES, TOLERANCE FROM THE INTOLERANT, AND KINDNESS FROM THE UNFRIENDLY

How do you identify the smartest or wisest person in the room? Look for the kindest one. Speaking about rooms, if you are the smartest in it, you are in the wrong one. In doubt, be humble and assume you are the least wise. Look to the input from the rest of the group to foster your own learning.

WE ARE ALL ONE

According to Albert Einstein, "Our separation from each other is an optical illusion."[12] And as Maxim Gorky professed, "Everything seems simple and near."[13] Don't forget a more lighthearted approach too: stop and pet a dog or a cat when you encounter one on the street.

CULTIVATE THE FOUR CARDINAL VIRTUES OF STOICISM

There is no problem or challenge so big that it can't be made better with these four virtues: courage, justice, self-control, and wisdom. In all our dealings in life, we must be courageous, we must be fair, we must be disciplined, and, above all, we must be wise. Hold yourself accountable for your actions and take time to reflect daily. After each day, ask yourself: What did I do well today? How can I do better tomorrow? By regularly scrutinizing yourself and reflecting on your actions, you will become more self-aware and more apt to live virtuously.

---

12 Albert Einstein, "Albert Einstein Quotes," Goodreads.com, accessed January 17, 2024, https://www.goodreads.com/quotes/169344-our-separation-from-each-other-is-an-optical-illusion.

13 Maxim Gorky, "Maxim Gorky Quotes," FancyQuote.com, accessed January 17, 2024, https://quotefancy.com/quote/2246259/Maxim-Gorky-Everything-seems-simple-and-near-Then-all-of-a-sudden-I-cannot-understand.

A GARDEN IS NOT TO SHOW

As Epictetus left us in his discourses, "If the grain sprouts before the stalk is fully developed, it will never ripen. That is the kind of plant you are, displaying the fruit too soon, and the winter will kill it."[14]

TRANSFORM THE FIVE PRINCIPLES OF THE DOJO KUN IN YOUR LIFE PHILOSOPHY

When I joined my friend's senseis in dojos around the world, the two moments I enjoy most of these meetings are the beginning and the end of every training, as we always begin and end meditating and remembering the principles of the Shotokan Dojo Kun. The principles are seek perfection of character, be faithful, strive for excellence, respect others, and refrain from violent behavior. Think creatively about how you can apply each of these to all areas of your life and make them your life philosophy.

LISTEN TO DIFFERENT MUSIC, READ MORE BOOK CATEGORIES, LEARN FROM OTHER CULTURES

I still remember the interesting sayings I learned from my Chinese friends when we lived in Indonesia and Singapore. Here are some of them:

- The tiger roars, the wind rises.
- No matter how high the mountain may be, it cannot crush the sun.
- Water is not purified simply by changing its course.

---

14   Ignacio Nieto Carvajal, "A Garden Is Not for Show," Daily Stoic, September 15, 2018, https://micropreneur.life/a-garden-is-not-for-show/.

- In a melon grove, do not tie your sandals (they will suspect you of picking melons); under a plum tree, do not adjust your cap (they will suspect you of picking plums).
- If you want happiness for an hour, take a nap. If you want happiness for a day, go fishing. If you want happiness for a year, inherit a fortune. If you want happiness for a lifetime, help somebody.
- A little impatience will spoil great plans.
- The shoe wears out the sock, the sock cannot wear out the shoe (it did not make a lot of sense for me either, just testing if you're paying attention!).

From our Korean partners, I learned the concept of "nunchi," which literally means "eye and body reading" and stresses the relevance of facial expressions and body language to get the fullest picture of what people really mean or to motivate them.

© Glasbergen/ glasbergen.com

"Your résumé is bloated with half-truths, false praise,
exaggeration and unsubstantiated accomplishments.
I'd like to hire you to write our Annual Report."

CHAPTER 3

IMPROVING SOCIETY ONE PERSON AT A TIME

When I was just starting school as a youth, I noticed something. I could run like the other children, and I could climb trees alongside them. At reading time, however, it seemed the other kids were able to make out the words easily. I didn't.

I had dyslexia, though as a child I didn't understand the exact condition or its symptoms. What I did know was that I wanted to read, too. In addition to my friends at school, I lived in a family where literacy and literature were highly valued. My father was a widely known sports journalist, and my mother worked in the publishing world.

While reading came naturally to so many, it seemed I would have to make an extra effort to achieve that goal. I tried different strategies to help the words on paper appear clearly in my mind. At one point, I held a text upside down and found I could better identify the words that way. In the end, I gave 120 percent, and eventually learned to read, just as I dreamt of.

Today, reading is part of my everyday routine, and I value the chance to learn from a wide variety of authors. I encourage my family to carry on this important tradition of reading, which leads to education. And growing in knowledge, in turn, is one way that we can help to improve society. Collectively, if we are looking for ways to learn, we can create better systems, stronger economies, and a better place for the next generation.

Through my reading dilemma in my childhood, I came to recognize that I had to give my 120 percent just to be average. Rather than getting down about that, though, I've used a similar concept in other areas of business and life. Sometimes we have to work harder than others to get a result. In those cases, I always ask, "Is it worth it?" For me, learning to read opened doors of opportunity throughout my childhood and well into my career. I have no regrets about having to dedicate so much time and energy to gain that skill.

For that reason, I now have a symbol that I like to use, which is Đ.

Allow me to explain. Reading the text in Spanish, "Đ" is akin to "dé más" or "give more" (along with a few other connotations). It reminds me to always do my best, and for this I keep track of my business and financial KPIs that are important to me. Most of all, I look for ways to impact as many people as possible in a positive way through my life and career (which alludes to the "+" or "más/more" sign). The symbol even reflects the approach I want to take. The straight part of the "D" reflects a desire to always stand up straight and have good posture. The curved portion of the letter indicates having a smile or approaching everything with a bit of fun.

I encourage you to do the same. Whether you create your own symbol that has meaning and guides your life, or you simply write down what's important to you, taking some time to focus on ways you can learn and improve can go a long way. You will be able to make better and more rational decisions. You'll be on the lookout to give your best, even if that means working harder than others. And most of all, if we all play our part, we can contribute to society and have a lasting impact.

In the following sections, I've included some tips and strategies to measure and improve your business performance, along with guidelines to increase your persistence and setting goals. As you read through them, ask yourself if you currently apply them in your life. You may find you already are carrying out a variation of some of these but could still add others to your daily life. After all, by reading and sharing, we can improve together.

MEASURING AND IMPROVING BUSINESS PERFORMANCE

EAT THE FROG FIRST

Start every day by completing the most uncomfortable task.

TO IMPROVE IT, MEASURE IT

The only way to progress is to measure your work from time to time. Personally and professionally speaking, create your scorecard with your own KPIs. In business, focus especially on measuring and improving the customer experience and satisfaction to drive enduring business success. As Michael Dell said, "What gets measured gets done."[15]

SET A VISION IN WRITING

You cannot reach a destination without first identifying one. Your reality will be the result of your vision. Once written, detail specific goals, steps, and tasks. Set completion dates for each of these. Do not forget that it is a lifetime project, so don't be in a hurry, pivot if necessary, and have fun with it.

BEING IN THE RACE IS MORE IMPORTANT THAN WINNING THE RACE

It is OK to win, but you will go much further learning from as many races as possible, as well as using failure as fuel for your next improvement.

TO PROGRESS, GET USED TO MAKING MISTAKES AND PARTICIPATING IN A TEAM

With every failure comes a great opportunity. Instead of getting frustrated and giving up when you fail, figure out where you need to improve and take the necessary steps to avoid making the same mistake again. As the African proverb says, "If you want to go fast, go alone. If you want to go far, go together." And as Sam Walton stated, "Individuals don't win, teams do."[16]

---

15   "Progress Made Real: How We Developed Our Most Ambitious Cultivating Inclusion 2030 Goals," Dell Technologies, 2020, https://www.delltechnologies.com/content/dam/delltechnologies/assets/corporate/pdf/progress-made-real-reports/delltech-nologies-cultivating-inclusion-goals-case-study.pdf.

16   "Sam Walton Quotes," QuoteFancy.com, accessed January 17, 2024, https://quote-fancy.com/quote/1459192/Sam-Walton-Individuals-don-t-win-in-business-teams-do#:~:text=%E2%80%9CIndividuals%20don't%20win%20in%20business%2C%20teams%20do.%E2%80%9D,-%E2%80%94%20Sam%20Walton.

SUCCESS IS ALWAYS COLLECTIVE

In the book *The Culture Code: The Secrets of Highly Successful Groups*, author Daniel Coyle visits a variety of diverse teams over a span of four years. He identifies what makes some cultures succeed and others fail. According to his findings, the three core skills necessary for developing highly successful teams are (1) building safety to generate bonds of belonging and identity, (2) sharing vulnerability to drive trust and cooperation, and (3) establishing purpose to build from shared goals and values.[17]

LEARN FROM OTHERS' MISTAKES AND DISCOVERIES

Whatever your goal in life, there is someone out there who has walked a similar path and taken notes.

START AND END MEETINGS ON TIME

And prepare for any meeting. Never go to a meeting or party empty-handed; have value to add, or a detail as a bottle or flowers to give. To make genuine connections with people, find out who they are or what their passions and interests are before meeting. Check places like LinkedIn or other social networks to learn more. Never end meetings without action items, even if they are only personal tasks.

CELEBRATE EVERY SMALL ADVANCE

We tend to focus on major milestones and overlook the value of smaller victories along the way. Even the smallest achievements are worthy of recognition and celebration. Moreover, giving recognition,

---

17   Daniel Coyle, "The Culture Code," DanielCoyle.com, accessed January 17, 2024, https://danielcoyle.com/the-culture-code/.

acknowledging, and celebrating these progresses strengthens our relationships with others.

THE MOST COMMON WEAKNESS OF SALESMEN IS THAT THEY ARE NOT PREPARED ENOUGH

They do not know the personal elements, hobbies, and pain points or needs of the customer. Also, in some cases, they are not confident or aggressive enough to ask for a sale or for the reason behind a "no."

ASK AND LISTEN; AVOID JUDGING OR CRITICIZING

For example, during performance reviews, ask your team members about their opinions on their performances. If you listen proactively, they will identify their gaps and learn through their own responses. Similarly with children, whenever we punish them, we are depriving them of the critical inner process of facing their own misbehavior. Ask them and give them time to go through this process. The world tells us loudly and often what they perceive as wrong from us. That is why one of our responsibilities as parents is to tell our children everything that they do right to feed their self-esteem, since to feel confident and secure is essential for success.

By the way, I'll take this opportunity to recognize that I committed a lot of mistakes with my daughters. After their early years, I read about how I should have listened to them with full attention, and stopped whatever I was doing to focus on them with a sympathetic silence rather than vomiting solutions immediately. I should have reinforced those many positive behaviors I was so proud of but never acknowledged. So, to my daughters, I'm sorry for not praising you as much as I should and for not sharing with you all those moments you impressed me and made me feel proud with your many good deeds, strengths, and virtues.

PERSISTENCE AND GOAL SETTING

YOU CAN ALWAYS PUSH A LITTLE HARDER THAN YOU THINK

Whenever your body can do no more, your mind and soul can. Whenever your mind is exhausted, your soul has a surplus of energy. My Krav Maga colleagues are constantly reminding me of the Navy SEALs' 40 percent rule: When your mind tells you that you're exhausted, fried, and totally tapped out, you're really only 40 percent done, you still have 60 percent left in your tank! I like to think of the athlete Diana Nyad, who at the age of sixty embarked on a nearly impossible lifelong dream. She wanted to swim from Cuba to Florida, across more than one hundred miles of open ocean. She accomplished this, and afterward she told others to never give up, that you're never too old to accomplish your dreams, and that it takes a team![18]

PUSH FORWARD, EVEN WHEN IT'S HARD

You will suffer, so choose something worth suffering for.

SET UP A PLAN IF YOU WANT TO LOSE WEIGHT

If you desire physical freedom and want to prevent health problems from bad habits, develop a routine of healthy eating and regular exercise. As Tony Robbins shares, "It's not true that skipping breakfast will make you lose weight, but skipping dinner might help in that regard." For a timeline, he adds, "It took more than a day to put it on. It will take more than a day to take it off."[19]

---

18   Nyad Film, *Nyad*, Netflix.com, https://www.netflix.com/gb/title/81447231.

19   Tony Robbins, *The Holy Grail of Investing* (New York: Simon & Schuster, 2024).

THINK BIG

As Azim Premji stated, "If people are not laughing at your goals, your goals are too small."[20]

GO AFTER ONE GOAL AT A TIME

As Confucius stated, "Whoever chases two rabbits catches neither."[21]

THE ROOT OF YOUR SUCCESS IS YOUR DAILY OR WEEKLY ROUTINE

You will change your life as soon as you change something critical you do daily (or in some cases, as you change your way of thinking or beliefs that are imprisoning you or weighing you down). Making one step in the right direction consistently exemplifies why it's more important to focus on the direction than the result. If you focus on doing one small thing right consistently, the results will show.

IF YOU LACK CONCRETION, YOU WILL LACK PROGRESSION

Clearly define your long-term goals, including those larger-scale desires that you can satisfy over time. For example, you might dream of traveling the world, starting a family, or creating a business. Like stars, this form of attention illuminates the chosen direction of movement.

---

20   Azim Premji, "Azim Premji Quotes," Goodreads.com, https://www.goodreads.com/quotes/3702226-if-people-are-not-laughing-at-your-goals-your-goals.

21   Confucius, "Quotes by Confucius," Goodreads.com, https://www.goodreads.com/quotes/8688305-the-man-who-chases-two-rabbits-catches-neither.

STRIVE TOWARD THE GOAL AS BEST YOU CAN

As Sylvester McNutt stated, "In life, the only things you can control are your effort and your attitude. Everything else is not up to you."[22]

BECOME MORE TO HAVE MORE

Success is something you attract by the person you become.

FIGHT WITH SMART RESILIENCE AND BE AWARE THAT LIFE IS A ROLLER COASTER

Enjoy it. There are no straight lines or shortcuts in this universe. Remember what Muhammad Ali noted in an interview: "I hate every minute of training, but I said, 'Don't quit.' Suffer now and live the rest of your life as a champion."[23]

PATIENCE IS A GOOD INGREDIENT OF ANY RECIPE

Some processes take time and cannot be rushed, especially value investing. Patience also fosters a sense of calmness and resilience. It allows us to approach situations with a level-headed perspective, making better decisions and avoiding impulsive actions.

JUST ASK FOR IT

Nike's "Just do it" is one of the best mottos in terms of proactivity. For results, I encourage "Just asking." Nine times out of ten, you'll receive a "no" to your request. However, the few times you hear "yes" will be worth it.

---

22   S. Mcnutt, "S. Mcnutt Quotes," Goodreads.com, https://www.goodreads.com/quotes/11634219-in-life-the-only-two-things-you-can-control-are.

23   Muhammad Ali, "Muhammad Ali Quotes," BrainyQuote.com, accessed January 17, 2024, https://www.brainyquote.com/quotes/muhammad_ali_148629.

DON'T GET EMOTIONAL—GET FOCUSED

The emotions we experience can be either pleasant or unpleasant, high energy or low energy. When we learn to manage them properly, we give ourselves a chance to experience life to the fullest. Expand your emotional vocabulary so you don't mistake one emotion for another and express these feelings so that you can enjoy true spiritual freedom. Talk about them with a friend or someone you can trust, or you can release your suppressed feelings through writing. Avoid defensiveness and embrace self-improvement. Instead of deflecting criticism or making excuses, be open to self-reflection and growth. Ignore, as much as possible, the irrelevant emotions that arise and are so easy to distract yourself with. Surround yourself with positive influences that can help you stay motivated and focused on your goal. Also, be in the present moment and engage in activities that bring you joy and fulfillment!

WHAT KIND OF BOXER ARE YOU?

As Mike Tyson pointed out, "Plans last only until you're punched in the face."[24] Are you going to leave the boxing ring as soon as you receive your first punches? In addition, Marcus Aurelius stated, "The art of living is more like wrestling than dancing, because an artful life requires being prepared to meet and withstand sudden and unexpected attacks."[25] Train yourself and your mind to adapt to any circumstance. You don't need to have the answer for every question or contingency. Adapt and change with the circumstances. Be resilient instead of rigid. Focus on the strategy rather than the tactics.

---

24 Ivan Luxenberg, "Stoic Lessons on Mental Health," LinkedIn, January 28, 2021. https://www.linkedin.com/pulse/stoic-lessons-mental-health-ivan-luxenberg/.

25 Daily Stoic, "Be Prepared for Sudden Attacks," DailyStoic.com, https://dailystoic.com/be-prepared-for-sudden-attacks/.

THERE IS ALWAYS MORE ROOM TO MANEUVER THAN INITIALLY THOUGHT

Remember how many times you thought you were certain to fail the test, but you managed to achieve a decent score? Reframe the problem, challenge some perceived rules or limitations, find a better problem to solve, or uncover overlooked pathways. There are always more options than initially expected.

ANYONE CAN GET LUCKY, ONLY FEW PERSEVERE

"God favors fools," according to the saying. It is true that anyone can get lucky, but only those who persevere through difficulties, hard work, and honesty are worthy of admiration and emulation.

NEVER GIVE UP

Slow and steady wins the race. Don't expect instant gratification when pursuing your goal; you're in it for the long run. The payoff will come in many ways, and it will last. As the Turkish proverb says, "There is no mountain without fog; no man of merit without slanderers."

IF YOU DON'T HAVE ANYTHING INTERESTING TO SHARE, DON'T CALL; IF YOU DO, CALL A HUNDRED TIMES

Never call on a prospect just to ask for an order. Wait to have something useful or informative to share.

READY, FIRE, AIM

In doubt, be action oriented. You can learn by trying something. That's enough. Any action is helpful even if it's not perfect. Consistent practice is the key to improvement.

IT'S NOT OVER TILL YOU QUIT

Winners don't quit when things don't go their way; they restrategize until they get it right. Delayed gratification increases your level of self-awareness and humility. And as US Army General Douglas MacArthur said, "Age wrinkles the body. Quitting wrinkles the soul."[26]

EMULATE THE TORTOISE, NOT THE HARE

Don't race against others; race against yourself. The key is to take firm steps looking ahead and enjoy the journey that is life. It's the journey that counts, not the destination. Life is a treasure, not a treasure hunt.

IF YOU TAKE A STEP BACK, YOU WILL TAKE TWO STEPS FORWARD SOON

Progress is not a smooth and continuous process. It involves periods of rapid advancement, followed by periods of consolidation or even regression. Looking back at my life, I notice a pattern of progress that includes both forward movement and setbacks and challenges that led to greater advancement in the long run. Remember that accomplishing a goal isn't always a straight path.

---

26   Douglas MacArthur, "Douglas MacArthur Quotes," Goodreads.com, accessed
       January 17, 2024, https://www.goodreads.com/author/quotes/317613.
       Douglas_MacArthur.

©Glasbergen / glasbergen.com

"Everyone has a purpose in life. My purpose
is to say NO whenever you ask for money."

CHAPTER 4

THE POWER OF FINDING PURPOSE

When I think about purpose, three words immediately come to mind. The first is illusion, in terms of living life with an enthusiastic, positive approach. The second is growth, as you can use your entire life to learn and become wiser. The third and final word is fulfillment, because if you are using your talents in your vocation, you'll likely feel more satisfaction.

If you've found your purpose in life, you'll usually see that these three concepts are present, too. You will be free of many of your previous fears and desires, you will have more energy, you'll be excited about gaining new information, and you'll be happy to carry out your duties. You'll likely be more resilient, as it will be easier to overcome challenges and get through the ups and downs. You'll be motivated to carry out what's important to you. Having a purpose can also reduce stress levels and create better physical and mental health.

For me, my purpose has always been to make a positive social impact, ideally a transgenerational one. I've traveled all over the world and learned from different cultures. I've observed how people act and what is important to them. I've chosen to go into business ventures based on how their models can help people today and tomorrow. For instance, my company Savia Capital stands for "Smarter Alternative Value-Added Investing Active Fund." Through Savia, we are assisting people in making an intelligent but also a positive impact use of their savings. We are showing them that using new technologies such as blockchain, decentralized finance (DeFi), and artificial intelligence (AI), which we'll cover more in-depth later, individuals can invest in new and smarter ways. They don't have to use a bank, pay high fees, or get denied access because of their income levels. Instead, they can have greater flexibility with how they use their savings and get higher returns and liquidity from their investments.

When I look back, one of the professional facets of which I am most proud of is the growth that Codere had during the ten years before its IPO, which allowed us to use the slogan 10×10, as we increased in those ten years ten times the revenues, the profits, and above all the number of employees. As a family company, it managed to employ more than twenty-one thousand workers and positively impacted their families, most of them being from Latin America.

I also especially enjoyed founding the Codere Foundation, and later, as president of Intralot, I continued to advise congressmen and senators to responsibly regulate new sports betting and lotteries products, and to dedicate all the taxes from these to scholarships.

Making a positive social impact is what motivates me every day to get up and go through my routines and habits to get in the right mindset. I work to be productive with my time and to always give my best effort. If I can help others invest in new ways that give them higher returns, they may be able to access more education and job opportunities and pay it forward thanks to this new financial peace or independence. They can have smarter choices for their savings and to improve their financial status. Doing this, they will also be able to free up their time and pursue other activities they enjoy or just enjoy more quality time with their loved ones.

If you've identified your purpose in life, you can read through the following sections to find additional tips. You might be able to tweak your current schedule or philosophy. If you haven't yet found your purpose, the quotes could help you brainstorm ideas. You may find you are drawn, like me, to helping others and making a difference for future generations.

FAITH AND SPIRITUALITY

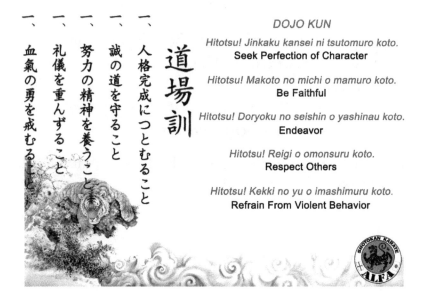

DOJO KUN

Hitotsu! Jinkaku kansei ni tsutomuro koto.
Seek Perfection of Character

Hitotsu! Makoto no michi o mamuro koto.
Be Faithful

Hitotsu! Doryoku no seishin o yashinau koto.
Endeavor

Hitotsu! Reigi o omonsuru koto.
Respect Others

Hitotsu! Kekki no yu o imashimuru koto.
Refrain From Violent Behavior

This is the Dojo Kun, a verbal affirmation that we always recite in our dojo at the beginning and end of each session.

GOD REQUIRES NOTHING FROM YOU

Get rid of the idea that you can secure God's favor through sacrifice.

GOD'S LOVE IS INFINITE AND UNCONDITIONAL

As in the parable of the prodigal son, there's always a way back, and He will always be there to welcome you.

ASK AND IT SHALL BE GIVEN TO YOU

Knock on God's door and He will open it.

MEMENTO MORI

This Latin phrase means "remember you will die." Don't take your days for granted and use your time wisely.

DO NOT EXPECT ANYTHING FROM OTHERS

We are here to serve, not to be served. Enjoy how you can positively impact more and more people with just small details such as smiles and sincere praises.

FORGIVE THEM—THEY DON'T KNOW

As Jesus said, "Father, forgive them, for they know not what they do" (Luke 23:34).[27]

---

27   Luke 23:34, https://www.unity.org/bible-interpretations/
     luke-2334-then-jesus-said-father-forgive-them-they-do-not-know-what-theyre.

ONE DAY IT ALL WILL MAKE SENSE

As Epictetus in his discourses reminds us, "Whenever you find yourself blaming providence, turn it around in your mind and you will see that what has happened is within reason."[28]

FAITH IS NOT BELIEVING WHAT WE DO NOT SEE—IT'S HOPING IN WHAT WE DON'T SEE

Skeptics say, "I'll believe it when I see it." Believers state, "I'll see it when I believe it."

TAKING A LEAP OF FAITH IS A WIN-WIN

Take scary action steps to improve your financial situation. If you nail it, good for you. If you don't, good for you, too—you will learn lessons. That's much better than staying stuck inside your comfort zone. In fact, in some cases, it is better to leap without a safety net than it is to live with inaction.

LIVE CELEBRATING THAT GOD IS INSIDE YOU

Judge no one and pray for others.

A STRONG SOUL IS BETTER THAN GOOD LUCK

Training your soul for any kind of luck, being ready and sturdy for the hard winters of life—that is the secret of the strongest.

---

28 Ignacio Nieto Carvajal, "One Day It Will All Make Sense," Micropreneur Life, March 13, 2018, https://micropreneur.life/daily-stoic-march-13th-one-day-it-will-all-make-sense/#:~:text=Ignacio%20Nieto%20Carvajal&text=%E2%80%9COne%20 day%20it%20will%20all,is%20in%20keeping%20with%20 reason.%E2%80%9D&text=Wow%2C%20it's%20amazing%20how%20 such,and%20ideas%20in%20my%20mind.

YOUR SOUL IS SAFE

Find peace and stability within yourself and seek the path that brings you fulfillment.

GOD HAS YOUR BACK

As Apollon Maykov reminds us, "The darker the night, the brighter the stars; the deeper the grief, the closer is God!"[29]

IT'S ALL ABOUT SHINING EYES

Do something noteworthy by Him. Ideally, massive action in line with His plan.

YOU NEVER FAIL GOD'S TESTS; YOU JUST KEEP TAKING THEM UNTIL YOU PASS

Live according to His standards, rather than society's.

This is my daily prayer before I go to sleep.

LIFE PURPOSE

SET ASIDE TIME TO DO WHAT YOU ENJOY

Use this time to disconnect from your duties and obligations. Don't underestimate the importance of forming close connections with others. By carving out this time, you'll give your life purpose a chance to emerge.

---

29 Danielle Dahl, "70 Late Night Quotes about What Goes on When the Sun Sets," Everyday Power, October 31, 2022, https://everydaypower.com/late-night-quotes/.

FIND YOUR FUNNIEST WAY TO SERVE OTHERS

Test different ways of being helpful to those around you and see what works best.

DISCOVER THE REAL REASON FOR BEING HERE AND THEN HAVE THE COURAGE TO ACT ON IT

And don't worry about the results.

YOU WERE CALLED TO DO SOMETHING THAT ONLY YOU CAN DO

Use your obstacles and circumstances to find your purpose and keep going.

YOUR WORK DONE WELL WILL OUTLIVE YOU—THAT'S YOUR LEGACY

My father, known to my daughters as *"el abuelito,"* used to say that work was his therapy. The best use of life is to use it for something that will outlast it. By writing his last newspaper column the day before his death, he left us an example worthy of emulation.

STOP BUYING MATERIAL THINGS JUST TO HIDE YOUR NONMEANINGFUL LIFE

Instead, dedicate more time to think about the work you would like to be remembered for after you die. If you keep searching, you will find it.

STAYING IN BUD IS ALWAYS MORE PAINFUL THAN FLOWERING

The more you take action on your promptings, the sooner you will find your purpose. It is never too late to be what you might have been.

Avoid being the "most people" of Oscar Wilde's quote, "Living is one of the rarest things. Most people just exist."[30] And be patient, since as the Bible says, "There is a time for everything, and a time for every purpose under heaven" (Ecclesiastes 3:1–8).[31]

TAKE A CALM APPROACH TO GETTING OLDER

As Joseph Murphy shared, "Age is not the flight of years; it is the dawn of wisdom in the mind of man."

LIFE'S PURPOSE IS LEARNING TO LOVE

Follow Saint Augustine's advice: "Love and do whatever you want,"[32] and remember to find ways to laugh or at least smile every day.

---

30   Oscar Wilde, "Oscar Wilde Quotes," Goodreads.com, https://www.goodreads. com/author/quotes/3565.Oscar_Wilde#:~:text=Oscar%20Wilde%20 Quotes&text=Be%20yourself%3B%20everyone%20else%20is%20already%20 taken.&text=To%20live%20is%20the%20rarest,people%20exist%2C%20that%20 is%20all.

31   Ecclesiastes 3:1–8, https://sementesdafe.com/en/bible-trivia/ the-time-for-all-things-verse/.

32   Saint Augustine, "Saint Augustine Quotes," QuoteFancy.com, https://quotefancy. com/quote/905913/Saint-Augustine-Love-and-do-what-you-want-If-you-stop- talking-you-will-stop-talking-with.

© Glasbergen/ glasbergen.com

"All of my professors told us the key to success is doing something you love. I love living at home with you and mom!"

CHAPTER 5

A PATH THAT LEADS TO GROWTH

I'm very careful about how I spend my time. I have a schedule that lays out what I will do during my working hours and shows how I will spend my leisure time. This is important to me because I know that to be the most productive, I have to focus on the right and most relevant tasks.

I've always been passionate about innovation, especially when it comes to using it for growth and to make a social impact. This means I am constantly reading all kinds of books and magazines as well as researching online to learn about advancements. I also need to spend time analyzing studies and shareholder letters to stay on top of changes. I'm especially aware of the real estate markets, the stocks in the S&P 500, Nasdaq 100 and Russell 2000, the private equity positions, art in general, and the new developments in AI, blockchain, and tokenization, which we'll discuss in more detail later.

In my free time, I look for start-ups that can do more with less and have the potential to create a significant long-term positive effect for society. I take time to listen to noteworthy podcasts and take care of my health and well-being. I engage in forest bathing, and participate in Krav Maga and karate dojos, where I have a sandan black belt sensei status. I watch films inspired by real events, play the clarinet and saxophone, and spend time with my family.

All of these commitments mean that I have to be rigorous with how I use every minute of the day. By prioritizing my efforts, I can continue to grow both professionally and personally, to live out my purpose, and to serve others. To help me remember what really matters, I've developed the acronym "FORS" (which is also my nickname). It stands for "Focus on Relationships and Service."

I suggest you take the same approach and look constantly for ways to improve. As you start out in your career, you'll be afraid of taking more risky or difficult steps. But as US Army General Norman Schwarzkopf said, "The more you sweat in peace, the less you bleed in war."[33]

Read through the following sections to learn what you might be able to do to be a high performer. You'll want to think about what success means to you, and how you can achieve those goals. Use these pieces of advice to fine-tune your plans, and remember, every day is an opportunity to test and grow (regardless of the results, you are learning).

---

33 Norman Schwarzkopf, "Norman Schwarzkopf Quotes," BrainyQuote.com, https://www.brainyquote.com/quotes/norman_schwarzkopf_455013.

PROFESSIONAL GROWTH AND SUCCESS

LEAVE YOUR IMAGINATION TO FLY

Give free rein to your imagination to envision ways in which you could create a positive impact in the world. Align those ideas with purposeful action to make your dreams of a better world a reality. Forget about what everybody thinks success means. What meaning do you ascribe to success?

SEEK A ROLE MODEL AND REVERSE-ENGINEER YOUR PLAN

Any career transition starts with believing in yourself and having a clear vision of where you want to go. Once you have identified this destination, seek out a mentor or role model in your desired field to provide insight and clarity, and strategically reverse-engineer a customized plan for yourself. Approach it in bite-sized chunks, focusing on daily disciplines, skill development, and relationship building that will move you incrementally toward your ultimate goal.

ALWAYS BE YOURSELF

As Henry David Thoreau wrote, "Be yourself, not your idea of what you think somebody else's idea of yourself should be."[34] You don't need to change or adapt to any society standard. As Bernard Baruch shared, "Be who you are and say what you feel because those who mind don't matter and those who matter don't mind."[35] Your success is your story, a work in progress, and you own it.

---

34   Henry David Thoreau, "Be Yourself," Let Yourself Learn, https://letyourselflearn. com/2013/10/22/be-yourself-not-your-idea-of-what-you-think-somebody-elses-idea-of-yourself-should-be-%E2%80%95-henry-david-thoreau/.

35   Bernard Baruch, "Bernard Baruch Quotes," Goodreads.com, https://www.goodreads. com/quotes/865-be-who-you-are-and-say-what-you-feel-because.

THE PURPOSE OF AN INTERNSHIP IS TO IDENTIFY IF YOU ARE SOMEONE THEY CAN TRUST

And if they would like to work with you.

ALL IN

Give it all, all the time. Approach each task as if it were your last because it very well could be. The sooner you begin to work the better.

SWEAT THE SMALL STUFF

Care about tiny details. Good work is the culmination of hundreds of tiny details. The world's most successful people sweat the small stuff.

THE OBSTACLE IS THE WAY

If something is hard, it is a chance to get stronger. Your mind is infinitely elastic and adaptable, so be ready for incremental challenges.

NO ONE SAID IT WOULD BE EASY

If doing good or launching businesses were easy, everyone would do it.

YOU ARE A START-UP, TOO

Like a start-up, you just began as an idea. You were "incubated" and put out into this world where you develop slowly, and over time you accumulate siblings, friends, and wellness, as in business you accumulate partners, employees, customers, investors, and wealth!

JUST DO IT

… if you love it, or if it is worth it. Fear is the enemy of growth, so if you're feeling it ask yourself how life could be without fearing the future. Life is short; do not let fear hold you back. In fact, I like the actionable version of the acronym FEAR: Face Everything and Rise. The attitude to fear is what separates those who aspire and those who achieve. Action is the antidote to fear. Every time in my life that I decided to face one of my fears, from being the second youngest in my IESE MBA class to developing new business projects in Indonesia, Singapore, Italy, and the United States that no one had tried before, I managed not only to expand my comfort zone but also to increase my self-complacency.

PUT IN THE HOURS

As American television host Jimmy Kimmel shared, "The only thing that I think I did right is that I always tried to work harder than anyone else."[36]

DEFINE WHO AND WHERE YOU WANT TO BE, THEN GIVE ONE STEP FORWARD DAILY UNTIL IT IS TRUE

The more specific the better. I smile remembering Lily Tomlin's thought, "I always wanted to be somebody. I should have been more specific."[37] Your principal handicap to arrive where you want will probably be your fear of other people's opinion but remember that your feelings should not depend on someone else's head thoughts. And be also aware of the people you surround yourself with, since to soar like an eagle it is not recommended to be surrounded by turkeys.

36   Jimmy Kimmel, "Jimmy Kimmel: The Hardest Working Person in Show Business," https://www.success.com/jimmy-kimmel-the-hardest-working-man-in-show-business/.

37   Lily Tomlin, "Lily Tomlin Quotes," BrainyQuote.com, https://www.brainyquote.com/quotes/lily_tomlin_109612.

SIMPLY SHOW UP

As Woody Allen said, "Eighty percent of success consists of being there."[38] Even if it is not your best or strongest day, it will help you to expand your comfort area. As Ross Perot put it, "Success depends on how we react to unexpected opportunities."[39] Avoid too much social networking. Focus just on "bridge networking"—that is, on connecting with equally creative minds or with those you can give or add value.

ON STAGE, AMUSE YOURSELF OR GO HOME

The audience smells if you are enjoying the process, which generates empathy and persuasion. On the contrary, if you go up on the stage with more fear than enjoyment, they will also perceive it, and it will be a waste of time and credibility.

KEEP LOOKING UP

According to Charlie Chaplin, "You'll never find a rainbow if you're looking down."[40]

FORGET THE SPOTLIGHT EFFECT

Don't worry about what others think of you. Don't be affected by the spotlight effect, the one that assumes people are paying more attention to you than they really are. The reality is that everyone has greater concerns, particularly themselves.

---

38   Woody Allen, "Woody Allen Quotes," BrainyQuote.com, https://www.brainyquote. com/quotes/woody_allen_145883.

39   Ross Perot, "Inspiring Life Quotes," Google Groups, https://groups.google.com/g/ phpprogrammers/c/CfC0kSyDlX8?pli=1.

40   Charlie Chaplin, "Charlie Chaplin Quotes," Goodreads.com, https://www.goodreads. com/quotes/77677-you-ll-never-find-a-rainbow-if-you-re-looking-down.

GIVE BACK TO THE COMMUNITY

Most successful people spend part of their time offering their knowledge, expertise, or resources; expanding their horizons; gaining new perspectives; and sharpening their abilities. Remember that what is not given is lost.

ATTITUDE IS BETTER THAN APTITUDE

Training kravate (Krav Maga + karate) with marshals, bodyguards, and Navy SEALs, I've learned that everyone prefers someone they can trust that will not leave them behind.

IN LIFE, YOU ONLY GET ONE TAKE

You never get a second chance to make a good first impression. Prepare for high-stakes conversations in advance, role-playing your lines, and running through the potential arguments and counterarguments in your head. You'll sound far more confident and authoritative during the real event if you're not stumbling over your words.

EVEN IF THE PROGRESS IS SLOW, KEEP AT IT

Honing a skill that you could expand into a future business is always a smart bet. The job market is more fragile than ever. To protect yourself against a future layoff, it's a good idea to consider side hustles—what could you invest in now that would generate income later on? Pick one or two things and then start, day by day, to get better at them. Steady progress toward your goals is the best strategy to achieve success and fulfillment. And remember that in our own journey to self-improvement: One never arrives. Success is a constant work in progress!

ALL GREATNESS COMES FROM CONSTANTLY EXPANDING YOUR COMFORT ZONE

Later, when all is well, you'll look back at the most difficult times in your life and be glad that you never gave up. The world is not designed for you to succeed, nor is the system. They are both designed for you to be average and to constantly tempt you to give up. Early in your career, your natural talent and motivation may have been enough. To keep moving forward, if you still think the job or business is for you, focus hard on doing what's most needed, even if that means building new skills or taking on unfamiliar roles.

JOIN OR CREATE A MASTERMIND GROUP

Two heads are better than one. Meet on a regular basis, and act as accountability partners, mentors, and mates to each other. CEOs and entrepreneurs in the United States working with mentors for three years or more experience an average EBITDA CAGR of 66 percent, which is more than five times the national average.

EVERYTHING IS NEGOTIABLE

Most negotiations stall before they've started because we don't realize a negotiation is possible. A salary offer is negotiable. The terms of your mortgage are negotiable. The seat you're assigned on an airplane is negotiable. Get in the habit of asking, "Is there room to negotiate here?" The results might surprise you. And remember, to negotiate successfully, we must learn to control our emotions, especially fear, anger, and worry. A calm and neutral attitude is best for negotiating. Friendliness is good for breaking the ice, but calmness is excellent for sealing the deal. As Robert Estabrook says, "He who has learned to disagree without being disagreeable has discovered the most valuable secret of negotiation."[41]

LOOK FOR THREE "YESES" TO CEMENT A DEAL

In the book *Never Split the Difference,* Chris Voss recommends using open-ended questions such as "How?" and "What?"[42] For example, ask "How should I do this?" to force the other person to solve the problem they imposed on you and to avoid escalation. Using these types of questions will help you get the three "yeses" from the other person. Agreeing to commit is the first "yes," labeling and summarizing their point is the second, and the "how" or "what" questions will provide the final "yes."

PREPARE THREE ALTERNATIVES AND A PROPOSAL

When suggesting a change or solution, always bring three alternatives and a proposal prepared in advance.

AS LONG AS YOU ARE TRYING YOUR HARDEST, YOU ARE ON THE RIGHT PATH

The path to achieving our aspirations is rarely straightforward, so focus on your own efforts and personal goals, rather than external comparisons or societal expectations.

41   Robert Estabrook, "Robert Estabrook Quotes," Goodreads.com, https://www.goodreads.com/quotes/501685-he-who-has-learned-to-disagree-without-being-disagreeable-has.

42   Chris Voss, *Never Split the Difference* (New York: Random House Business, 2017).

IT'S A NUMBERS GAME

First, you cannot win the lottery if you do not buy a ticket. Second, invest your time and money in businesses or investments with much better odds than the lottery.

CHOOSE A JOB OR BUSINESS THAT MATCHES YOUR UNIQUE TALENTS AND SKILLS

Don't pick the job with the highest salary attached, but the one that matches your unique talents and skills and fires you up. Once there, be creative, proactive, patient, and unconventional.

WORK ON YOUR SYSTEMS AND GOALS

Avoid luring distractions and follow weekly KPIs or monthly OKRs (objectives and key results). Achieve quick wins and celebrate every progress point and milestone.

BE A SOLUTIONS GIVER VERSUS A PROBLEMS POINTER

In the same way that people love to buy rather than being sold, people love doers over excuse makers. Also, everyone loves enthusiastic people over complainers or whiners.

CHOOSE GOALS MUCH BIGGER THAN YOU AND WRITE THEM DOWN

The key to success lies in deciding on what you truly want, writing your desires down, and coming up with a detailed plan to fulfill your purpose. You'll also need a positive mindset, great time management skills, and a willingness to keep failing until you get it right.

PROCRASTINATION TODAY WILL MAKE TOMORROW MORE COMPLICATED

Think about the consequences of putting something off to help you avoid procrastination.

NO PAIN, NO GAIN

Broaden your comfort area. People with a low tolerance for risk, or who are guided by fear, have a low propensity for success.

EVERY DAY THAT YOU ARE NOT GETTING BETTER, YOU ARE GETTING WORSE

Most of the time, it is just learning new things about your profession or business. As Abraham Lincoln stated, "Give me six hours to chop down a tree and I will spend the first four sharpening the ax."[43] And as St. Augustine also stated, "Know thyself, accept thyself, overcome thyself"[44] (I would add "constantly").

NEVER REGRET YOUR DECISIONS

Apologize if needed and keep moving forward. Beware of the attribution bias, whereby we attribute successes to our own abilities and failures to chance. Remember that people are motivated by either avoiding a loss or acquiring a potential gain, and according to psychologists we value avoiding a loss up to three times more than a potential gain!

---

43   Abraham Lincoln, "Abraham Lincoln Quotes," Goodreads.com, https://www.goodreads.com/quotes/search?q=give+me+six+hours+to+chop+down+a+tree.

44   Matthew Drever, *Know Thyself!* (Oxford: Oxford Academic, 2013), https://academic.oup.com/book/26336/chapter/194626568.

YOU WILL REGRET THINGS YOU DIDN'T DO MORE THAN MISTAKES YOU MADE

The move you didn't make, the career change you didn't make, the business you didn't start … You will especially regret the times you didn't take a chance on yourself.

FOLLOW THE TWENTY-ONE-MINUTE RULE

Try to never eat alone and spend at least twenty-one minutes eating your meals. There's no point rushing.

FOLLOW THE FIVE-HOUR RULE

Like Bill Gates or Elon Musk, spend five hours a week learning something new.[45]

MEDITATE, EXERCISE, WRITE, AND READ EVERY DAY

Meditate or pray, stay healthy, and read things like summaries from *Blinkist* or *Headway* to learn from the experiences of others—it's quicker and cheaper!

TAKE LIFE AS IF YOU WERE CLIMBING MOUNT EVEREST

Climbers do not look up or down. They just focus on the next step. And if bored, think of Indira Gandhi's insightful memory: "My grand-father once told me that there were two kinds of people: those who

---

45   Sounak Mukhopadhyay, "5-Hour Rule: The Secret Sauce to Success for Elon Musk, Bill Gates," Mint.com, August 16, 2022, https://www.livemint.com/news/world/5hour-rule-the-secret-sauce-to-success-for-elon-musk-bill-gates-11660546762174.html.

do the work and those who take the credit. He told me to try to be in the first group; there was much less competition."[46]

WHAT YOU ALLOW IN YOUR BRAIN WILL BE REFLECTED IN YOUR LIFE

If you allow negative, self-limiting, or destructive thoughts to dominate your thinking, it will hinder your progress and impede your ability to reach your full potential. On the other hand, by consciously selecting empowering thoughts and beliefs, you will create a ripple effect that will positively impact your actions, decisions, and overall well-being.

PRACTICE VISUALIZATION

Visualize the perfect performance, enjoy the imperfect one, and repeat. Do the same with goals, having in mind George Bernard Shaw's recommendation: "Look for the circumstances and if you don't find them, make them."[47] In other words, don't search for success—live it!

PERFECT IS THE ENEMY OF THE GOOD

Focus on excellence rather than perfectionism. Excellence is doing the best possible with the available resources and circumstances of the moment. Expect excellence from your team and reward the same. Talent is not the cause of excellence—practice is. Focus on incremental steps rather than dramatic moves. For example, try a trial period at a new job before you fully commit. Celebrate progress versus perfection.

---

46   Indira Gandhi, "There Are Two Kinds of People," Quote Investigator, https://quoteinvestigator.com/2013/11/20/work-credit/.

47   George Bernard Shaw, "George Bernard Quotes," Goodreads.com, https://www.goodreads.com/quotes/39982-people-are-always-blaming-their-circumstances-for-what-they-are.

BUILD AND MAINTAIN A STRONG "NETWORK OF LUCK"

In his book titled *Chase, Chance, and Creativity: The Lucky Art of Novelty*, neurologist Dr. James Austin identifies four types of luck: blind luck, luck from motion, luck from awareness, and luck from uniqueness.[48] He recommends that when facing two paths, choose the path that has a larger "luck surface area" (basically, it's hard to get lucky watching TV at home—it's easy to get lucky when you're engaging, learning, writing or sharing in public, and spending time in rooms where you feel like the least wise person).

GET A PERSONAL COACH AND IDENTIFY SEVERAL MENTORS TO APPROACH WHEN NEEDED

The best golfers know how to swing a golf club; still, they practice and have a trainer or coach who reminds them how to optimize it. Regarding mentors, none of them are perfect, but they all know something you don't, and that something can make a big difference. And remember, humility is the first requirement for mentorship.

BECOME AN EXPERT IN WHAT YOU ARE GOOD AT

Become an expert in whatever area or niche you flow. Focus on your strengths at least 70 percent of the time and develop them. Work constantly on yourself since you are your greatest asset. If you do what you love, and have fun, money will follow (in most cases) and if not, remember the highest, most satisfying experiences in people's lives are when we are in flow.

---

48   James H. Austin, *Chase, Chance, and Creativity: The Lucky Art of Novelty* (New York: MIT Press, 2003).

LET OTHERS JUDGE YOU BY THE ENEMIES YOU MADE

If nobody hates you, nobody knows you. As witty Oscar Wilde left written, "The only thing worse than being talked about is not being talked about."[49] And never play the role of the sheep or you will get slaughtered.

THE LESS YOU TALK, THE SMARTER YOU APPEAR

If you are not an expert or you are not prepared, you have no place else to go but down by talking. Remember that according to researchers, words convey only 7 percent of the message, while voice and body language convey 38 percent and 55 percent, respectively.[50] Therefore, be present, smart, and use your natural skills of empathy, understanding, attentiveness, and kindness, as well as the many tools for building rapport, such as paying attention to their words, sharing their values or interests, and reassuring their concerns. These tools can break the ice and help us benefit each other.

TO LEARN, BE HUMBLE

Everyone is smarter, more successful, and wiser than us in something. Ralph Waldo Emerson put it well: "Every man I meet is my master at some point, and in that I learn of him."[51]

---

49   Oscar Wilde, "Oscar Wilde Quotes," National Library of Medicine, https://pubmed. ncbi.nlm.nih.gov/23688658/.

50   MasterClass, "How to Use the 7-38-55 Rule to Negotiate Effectively," July 7, 2021, https://www.masterclass.com/articles/ how-to-use-the-7-38-55-rule-to-negotiate-effectively.

51   "Ralph Waldo Emerson Quotes," Goodreads.com, https://www.goodreads.com/ quotes/8468-in-my-walks-every-man-i-meet-is-my-superior.

FOR NEGOTIATING IN GENERAL, NEVER ACCEPT A FIRST OFFER

Just say no and move on to negotiate.

BE PUNCTUAL

First, because it is a sign of a professional and educated person, and second, because you can prepare and review the arguments and objectives of the meeting. I resonate a lot with Admiral Lord Nelson's quote: "I owe much of my success to arriving a quarter of an hour before the appointed time."[52]

LISTEN TO EVERYONE TO LEARN THE TRUTH

I love the Argentine proverb, "He who speaks sows, he who listens reaps."[53] Listen more than you talk. To proactively listen or assist others to share their opinions, you can always make use of the question "How so?" or say, "Tell me more."

BOSSES' MINDS WORK IN A PECULIAR WAY

If you share a disruptive proposal, most bosses will hear the first time but won't listen. After you share it again, they will listen but won't understand. Finally, if you persevere, they will finish by understanding, taking your idea, and making it theirs.

---

52 Horatio Nelson, "Horatio Nelson Quotes," FancyQuote.com, https://quotefancy.com/quote/1342017/Horatio-Nelson-I-owe-all-my-success-in-life-to-having-been-always-a-quarter-of-an-hour.

53 "Who Speaks, Sows; Who Listens, Reaps," SlideServe, July 15, 2014, https://www.slideserve.com/eldora/who-speaks-sows-who-listens-reaps-argentine-proverb.

ATTEND CONFERENCES, SEMINARS, AND SIMILAR EVENTS

Even better, endeavor to be a speaker. Be someone worth talking to—be ready to share anecdotes from your last trip, hobbies, and/or businesses. Trust the serendipity of these meetings. Connecting with people increases your chances of getting new and exciting jobs, partners, or business ideas.

THE MINIMUM THREE HOURS RULE

You need to interact face-to-face for a minimum of three hours with someone to build confidence and get that person to invest in you or your company. So, be prepared to attend a minimum of one event per month or to invite someone out per week if you want to acquire new VIP customers or investors.

A WARM INTRO IS WORTH TEN COLD CALLS

From time to time, host get-together events. Keep it simple, don't be formal, create an atmosphere that shows that the event is for enjoyment, and mix and match as many guests as possible. If it's not possible to be face-to-face, be available to introduce your friends to whoever they need or you think would help them via email or LinkedIn when the opportunity arises.

SUCCESS IS A STATE OF MIND; IT HAS NOTHING TO DO WITH YOUR PRESENT LEVEL OF FINANCIAL ASSETS

So be careful what you allow in your brain. It will affect everything in your life. Additionally, financial success shouldn't overshadow personal fulfillment. You need a balance between personal growth and business success.

DON'T PUT OFF TASKS

As Walt Disney said, "The way to get started is to quit talking and begin doing."[54] And Abraham Lincoln added, "Discipline is choosing between what you want now and what you want most."[55]

ASK, ESPECIALLY IF THERE IS SOMETHING TO GAIN AND NOTHING TO LOSE

Ask smart questions and listen to feedback on your performance. An embarrassing moment happened to me in my preuniversity studies. In front of the whole class, a professor compared me to the number one student (who had straight As), indicating that I would still be more successful in life. At that moment, I listened in astonishment and blushed because I didn't know what he saw in me. Sometime later, I regretted not asking him to clarify his reasons. Today, I do not know if my other colleague is more successful or not (who knows what success means for my classmate or professor), and sincerely I don't care. I bring it up to remind you of not wasting any opportunity to get constructive performance feedback!

IF YOU ARE INVITED TO A MEETING, BE PREPARED TO SHARE HOW YOU SOLVED A PROBLEM, NOT WHAT HANDICAPS YOU FOUND

Those who have worked with me know my prerogative of "three alternatives and one proposal" as a necessary condition to start a conversation about any problem that arises. But it is not enough—to really stand out, you have to be proactive and ready to share how you already

---

54   Walt Disney, "Walt Disney Quotes," BrainyQuote.com, https://www.brainyquote.com/quotes/walt_disney_131640.

55   Abraham Lincoln, "Abraham Lincoln Quotes," Goodreads.com, https://www.goodreads.com/quotes/10466454-discipline-is-choosing-between-what-you-want-now-and-what.

solved the problem. As if it were a chess board, come with the next two or three moves already made to differentiate you from the 90 percent who will pause and will wait for their boss's instructions when a minor inconvenience arises.

CONSIDER IF IT'S BETTER TO ASK FORGIVENESS THAN PERMISSION

In most cases, seeking permission or collaboration may be the more prudent course of action. However, at other times, if you have a well-thought-out idea or action that can bring positive results, it might be worth proceeding with it even if you haven't obtained explicit permission.

IF INTERVIEWED, KEEP YOUR ANSWERS BRIEF AND SIMPLE

And be real, humble, and vulnerable (if not, you could appear too perfect or annoying).

GET MASSIVE ATTENTION, WHETHER THE AUDIENCE LIKES OR HATES YOU

Doing so will increase your odds of getting noticed by the right people. Stay proactive, humble, forgiving, and honest about your mistakes, and your talents and efforts will be sooner or later recognized.

STRENGTHEN YOUR MUSCLE OF EXCELLENCE AT THE SLIGHTEST OPPORTUNITY

For example, when you use a public establishment such as a library, or someone lends you something, leave it or return it better than it was before. Always run the last mile.

YOU DON'T HAVE TO BE BRILLIANT

Only a little bit wiser than others, on average, for a long time. Acknowledge the fact that you're not better than anyone else. Focus instead on growing and being better than your last standard.

ROME WASN'T BUILT IN A DAY

And they made a lot of mistakes building it! Failure is an opportunity to brave the weather and grow stronger.

YOUR PROFESSIONAL OR BUSINESS GROWTH IS NOT A LIFE SENTENCE

Balancing work and personal life is essential for finding meaning and fulfillment. Set boundaries, manage your time effectively, and continuously evaluate and adjust since work–life balance is not a one-time achievement but an ongoing process. Don't burn the candle at both ends.

BE AN EARLY RISER WITH ROUTINES

Adopt several important morning routines like meditation or working out, spending quality time with your family over breakfast, or reading up on the newest trends in your professional sphere. In the morning, our willpower is much stronger than in the evening. Thus, the wee, predawn hours are the best time to improve your life.

KEEP A LONG-TERM MINDSET

Don't expect instant gratification when pursuing your goal; you're in it for the long run.

THINK ONE FOOT FORWARD, AGAIN AND AGAIN

Any action is helpful, even if it's not perfect. Consistent practice is the key to improvement.

BUSINESS STRATEGIES AND GROWTH

EMBRACE THE UNFAMILIAR

Your comfort zone is holding you back—keeping you from doing what you have to do. Networking, growing, investing … these will constantly stretch your comfort zone.

BREAK THE RULES

Change the paradigm. Innovation happens when you push the boundaries, and on some occasions, you need to break them to improve your customers' experience or satisfaction. Constantly ask yourself how you might improve the user experience or make it more fun. What got you here may not get you there.

TAKE MASSIVE ACTION

This is the most important habit to grow. You've got to make it happen. The world is changed by your actions, not by your opinions and thoughts.

ASK YOUR CUSTOMERS WHAT SIMILAR PRODUCTS THEY ARE BUYING

Make a deal or buy up that rival. Loyal customers turn down better products and lower prices because they have a sentimental attachment to your company. Don't try to manipulate people into loving your brand; instead, focus on creating brand experiences that people want to be associated with.

TIME IS PRECIOUS, SO MAKE EVERY MINUTE WITH YOUR CLIENTS COUNT

Give the best possible service, especially to your VIP clients.

TRY AND TEST SOMETHING NEW DAILY

Use trial and error to find the way. A major error is often inches away from a breakthrough discovery. Just never commit the same mistake twice.

FOLLOW THE 70/30 PHILOSOPHY OF DECISION-MAKING

If you can predict that a decision has at least a 70 percent chance at success, you should go for it.

ALWAYS GET AT LEAST THREE QUOTES FOR WORK BEING DONE

And never accept the first quote you get.

NONE OF US ARE AS SMART AS ALL OF US

We can often come up with better solutions when we work together as a group. However, it's also wise to have a balance, and not bring in so many people that we lose direction. For instance, brainstorming is usually more efficient in groups of four or fewer.

CREATE A SENSE OF URGENCY

Avoid "stay-the-course" messages that won't energize people. Instead communicate a need for action.

UNDER-PROMISE AND OVER-DELIVER

And always leave room for unexpected events. Do what you say you will do. Be seen as someone with something to teach or share. Always sell to the customer "their" idea.

MAINTAIN AN EAGLE-EYED FOCUS ON CUSTOMERS OR GO HOME

Customer-centric focus has been the fuel of successful companies such as Amazon, Alphabet, and Dell. Always keep this principle in mind and look for ways to make use of technology to increase the customer's satisfaction and experience.

KEEP THINGS SIMPLE

As Max Amsterdam described it, "Business is the art of extracting money from another man's pocket without resorting to violence."[56] The simpler the better.

NO COMPANY WILL SURVIVE WITH JUST GOOD PEOPLE

It needs people who are crazy for constantly improving. To be the best in your industry, you need to be good at a variety of complementary skills that your customers value and that your competitors lack. As the famous journalist Emilio Romero used to hawk among his employees, we should surprise our customers and displease our competitors daily.

SYSTEMATIZE OR DIE

If you do not systematize your business processes, the value of your business will be zero. Systematize everything, including the perfor-

---

56 Max Amsterdam, "Max Amsterdam Quotation," EnglishClub, https://www.english-club.com/ref/esl/Quotes/Money/Business_is_the_art_of_extracting_money_from_another_man_s_pocket_without_resorting_to_violence._2728.php.

mance reviews of your team and name each of these processes to give them the relevance they deserve.

HOCKEY STICK EXPONENTIAL INCOMES COME FROM PREVIOUS ACCUMULATED LEARNING

Additionally, lifelong learning is the fountain of youth. Henry Ford said, "Anyone who stops learning is old, whether at twenty or eighty. Anyone who keeps learning stays young."[57]

COMPANIES HAVE NO SOUL

Elon Musk said, "Don't attach yourself to a person, place, or organization. Attach yourself to a mission, a calling, or a purpose. That's how you keep your power and your peace."[58]

---

57   "Never Stop Learning," Cranfield School of Management, https://blog.som.cranfield.ac.uk/execdev/never-stop-learning.

58   Livemint, "Elon Musk Valuable Advice Shared by Billionaire," Mint, August 22, 2022, https://www.livemint.com/news/world/elon-musk-valuable-advice-shared-by-billionaire-don-t-attach-yourself-harsh-goenka-11661140702271.html.

©Glasbergen / glasbergen.com

"Because a large font makes profits look bigger."

CHAPTER 6

A LENS TO SPOT OPPORTUNITIES

In 1969, pictures were taken of the astronauts preparing to take off for the moon. These photos show what they were planning to bring. The astronauts stood next to huge suitcases filled with the items they thought they would need.

Surprisingly, these heavy suitcases looked like large boxes. None of them had the wheels we often associate with luggage today. It would be another year before Bernard Sadow innovated travel with a model of a traditional suitcase on wheels attached to a long strap.[59]

Think about that for a moment. We sent people to the moon before we discovered suitcases could have wheels. The wheel of course had been invented by then, and so had suitcases. What was missing until that point was a person who would look at the problem of transporting a suitcase in a new way. This person broke the rules that

---

59 Beth Collier, "When Did Suitcases Get Wheels?" Curious Minds, January 6, 2023, https://bethcollier.substack.com/p/when-did-suitcases-get-wheels.

had been in place for travel and thought of a better way to serve the user. The process led to suitcases with wheels.

Today, of course, suitcases with wheels are sold widely around the world, and have greatly improved the traveler's experience. They're an example of how taking the time to be curious and look at ways to relieve pain points for consumers can lead to innovations. Successful entrepreneurship takes the customer's perspective and listens to what they are going through. The products and services that come from dedicating time for testing and gathering feedback have the potential to be exactly what consumers want and are willing to pay for.

That's the approach I've always taken as an entrepreneur. When I was in college, I got involved in my first start-up, and the company's objective was related to what I was studying at the time. It focused on getting investors to contribute to investment funds. However, rather than try to share how great the company was, I shifted the focus to the consumer. I made everything center around them and their experience, including the questions they wanted answered and the benefits they would receive. At the time, this approach was very different from the traditional sales tactics. But it took off, as many customers appreciated being in the middle of everything and I managed to become the fund's biggest seller of shares. I had broken the rules, and it had paid off.

If you're thinking about being an entrepreneur, remember that the journey typically starts with identifying an idea. You can then create a minimum viable product to see its potential in the market. Once you've found people who are interested in paying for it, you can build a team to fully create it and launch it into the market.

It may sound simple, but entrepreneurship requires leadership that's very focused and dedicated. Be prepared to get a huge number of rejections, which doesn't necessarily mean your idea is wrong; in some cases, it just means you haven't found your people or the right time for the market yet. Similarly, many times a "no" is not a refusal but a need for further dialogue to know more about the real reasons behind that first "no."

To stay motivated, I always recommend looking to start or invest in businesses that align with the change you want to see. You might get involved in a company that is working to democratize financial services, for instance. Or you could help fight against endemic diseases, hunger, and poverty in places where resources are not widely accessible. As Mahatma Gandhi recommended, "Be the change you want to see in the world."[60]

In your search, look for blue oceans instead of fighting red ones. A red ocean refers to a market that is already full of competitors. A blue ocean is a market that is yet to be discovered and isn't full of other players already. And remember that regardless of the color of the ocean, you will suffer, so choose something worth suffering for.

When launching a start-up, also make sure it has five key characteristics. The first of these involves solving a real pain with a creative techy solution. Check that leverage and scalability are possible. Finally, you'll want it to have an international strategy and to be purpose-driven.

I've always looked for ways to do things differently to improve the lives of others. I often think of how Jeff Bezos started Amazon when books were being sold in stores. He broke the rules, thought outside the box, and took a risk. Today, most consumers all over the world purchase books with a "click" rather than visit a store.

One of the advantages of entrepreneurship is that the more value you add, the greater your potential to impact and to build sustain-

---

60   Mahatma Gandhi, "Mahatma Gandhi Quotes," BrainyQuote.com, https://www.brainyquote.com/quotes/mahatma_gandhi_109075.

able revenue streams. As you read through the following quotes and explanations on entrepreneurship, set aside some time to think about your own interests. What do you think is missing in the world? How could you help consumers solve problems you also have? Once you've identified what you want to do, create strategies and a minimum viable team to stay motivated. If you are hoping to help the world, as I am always looking to do, you'll find it's easier to get through the low points with partners sharing the mission of the company, so together you can build a better tomorrow for yourself and others.

ENTREPRENEURSHIP

NEVER START A COMPANY ONLY TO EARN MONEY

Create a cause, not a business. Make something you believe in with a vision to positively impact people. Its "raison d'être" (reason for existing) has to be worth the sacrifices and suffering you will endure along the way. Also remember Elon Musk's advice: "If you aren't solving a real problem, a problem people will be happy to pay to have solved, you won't have a business, at least not for long."[61]

BE READY TO MAKE DECISIONS AND FOLLOW THROUGH

As Naval Ravikant shared, "If you cannot decide, the answer is 'no.'"[62]

---

61   Jeff Haden, "Elon Musk Says Living a Happy, Successful, and Meaningful Life Comes Down to 4 Simple Things," Inc.com, September 15, 2023, https://www.inc.com/jeff-haden/elon-musk-says-living-a-happy-successful-meaningful-life-comes-down-to-4-simple-things.html.

62   Thomas Waschenfelder, "The Decision Making Process: Make Obvious Decisions," https://www.wealest.com/articles/decision-making-process#:~:text=You%20don't%20want%20to,society%20is%20full%20of%20options.

IF YOU ARE GOING TO LAUNCH A BUSINESS, THE SOONER THE BETTER

As you get older, your savings and expertise may increase but so will your obligations. If you're unsure where to begin, make a list of three things that you find joy in, or think about how you could solve any current problem or pain you are suffering.

PREPARE TO PARTNER

Look for people whose strengths complement your weaknesses. In particular, partner with those who can optimize your customers' satisfaction. The better the user experience you can create on your website or app, the greater chance that more people will want to use it.

THE BEST PREDICTOR OF FUTURE BEHAVIOR IS PAST BEHAVIOR

Do due diligence on businesses before you invest in them or buy them. Also check the background of people, especially partners or critical employees.

GET UP AND DO SOMETHING

As Mark Zuckerberg stated, "The biggest risk is not taking any risk. In a world that is changing quickly, the only strategy that is guaranteed to fail is not taking risks."[63]

DON'T TRUST YOUR GUT

As I once read in a *Harvard Business Review* article, while intuition can be a powerful decision-making tool, it can be unreliable in complex

---

63   Mark Zuckerberg, "Mark Zuckerberg Wuotes," BrainyQuote.com, https://www. brainyquote.com/quotes/mark_zuckerberg_453450.

and unfamiliar situations.[64] Intuition is based on our experience and knowledge, so it's not always accurate. When making relevant decisions such as starting a business or facing unprecedented challenges, it is wiser to combine instinct, rational thinking, and careful analysis supported by AI and other relevant technologies.

LOVE WHAT YOU DO

If you love what you are doing, you will be successful. And there is also my mother's advice. She noticed the lack of diligence from the owner's son at the neighborhood grocery and said, "Don't open a fruit store if you don't like fruits."

GOOD BUSINESS IDEAS COME FROM GOOD QUESTIONS

When looking for business ideas, consider the question Jeff Bezos asks, "What's not going to change in the next ten years?" Or my question for identifying transcendental businesses, "What change today would positively impact people for at least two generations?"

ENTREPRENEURSHIP IS NOT FOR THE FAINTHEARTED

It's for those who are willing to do something now, to endure the setbacks, the ups and downs, and the rejections to make their dream a reality. As the saying goes, "If you can't stand the heat, get out of the kitchen." Move fast or get out of the way. And remember that the sport of business is the ultimate competition: 7 days a week × 24 hours a day × forever.

---

64 Eric Bonabeau, "Don't Trust Your Gut," *Harvard Business Review*, May 2003, https:// hbr.org/2003/05/dont-trust-your-gut.

LIVE A FEW YEARS OF YOUR LIFE LIKE MOST PEOPLE WON'T SO THAT YOU CAN SPEND THE REST OF YOUR LIFE LIKE MOST PEOPLE CAN'T

Entrepreneurs create their own paths and often enjoy a life of prosperity. It's also wise to live each day as if it is your last.

KEEP WORKING HARD, EVEN DURING TOUGH TIMES

Your efforts could pay off. Nelson Mandela shared, "It always seems impossible until it is done."[65]

CONSIDER DEDICATING A FEW YEARS TO BUILD A BUSINESS VERSUS SPENDING A LIFETIME CREATING IT FOR SOMEONE ELSE

As Kevin O'Leary said, "Nobody forces you to work at Walmart. Start your own business! Sell something to Walmart!"[66] And if you think that building a business is too risky, remember the saying of Jeff Bezos: "Given a 10 percent chance of a one hundred times payoff, you should take that bet every time."[67]

THE VALUE OF ENTREPRENEURSHIP CAN'T BE MEASURED

Would you rather make $300,000 a year and work all the time, or make $150,000 a year and do whatever you love at the time you positively impact the world?

---

65 Nelson Mandela, "Nelson Mandela Quotes," BrainyQuote.com, https://www.brainyquote.com/quotes/nelson_mandela_378967.

66 Kevin O'Leary, "Kevin O'Leary Quotes," BrainyQuote.com, https://www.brainyquote.com/authors/kevin-oleary-quotes#:~:text=Nobody%20forces%20you%20to%20work,Sell%20something%20to%20Wal%2DMart!&text=I'd%20rather%20invest%20in,assumes%20success%20from%20day%20one.

67 Jeff Bezos, "Jeff Bezos Quotes," Goodreads.com, https://www.goodreads.com/quotes/11111661-one-area-where-i-think-we-are-especially-distinctive-is.

DON'T BELIEVE WHEN OTHERS TELL YOU THAT YOU CAN'T DO WHAT THEY CAN'T DO

There will come times in your life when you will have to prove your real worth. Exceed others' expectations and have a sense of urgency to get the right tasks done.

WHEN THE STUDENT IS READY, THE TEACHER APPEARS

Similarly, when the entrepreneur is ready, the start-up idea appears. Nobody forces you to work at a department store, bank, or consulting firm. You could choose to start your own business and become a supplier for them.

DON'T BE AFRAID TO INNOVATE; BE DIFFERENT

You don't have to do what others are doing just because you want to feel like you belong. Dare to stand out.

THOSE WHO CAN, BUILD A START-UP; THOSE WHO CAN'T, CRITICIZE

We have to admit that entrepreneurs have a mix of passion, courage, resilience, and a dash of healthy insanity.

HE WHO DOES NOT RISK DOES NOT CROSS THE SEA

Keep this sailor's proverb in mind to move forward, assuming you've carried out a risk analysis and decided to proceed. As André Gide, a Nobel Prize–winning author, believed, "Man cannot discover new oceans unless he has the courage to lose sight of the shore."[68] And speaking of nautical metaphors, if you are afraid of how to start,

---

[68] André Gide, "André Gide Quotes," BrainyQuote.com, https://www.brainyquote.com/quotes/andre_gide_120088.

remember that the British defeated the Spanish Armada because they had smaller, faster, and more flexible ships.

ALWAYS CONSIDER THE US MARKET FOR YOUR PRODUCT OR SERVICE

Regardless of where you are located, keep in mind that the United States has high levels of consumption and could be open to what you are selling.

BEWARE OF ESPECIALLY COMPLEX INDUSTRIES OR BUSINESSES

Invest in businesses with profits, easy-to-understand cash flow, and places where you can add value. As Sir Richard Branson warned, "If you want to be a millionaire, start with a billion dollars and launch an airline."[69]

ALWAYS WEAR THE PRO-UNICORN BINOCULARS

Keep your radar open for prospecting businesses to set up or invest in that comply with the five rules of all unicorns: they need to have the capacity to be leveraged, be scalable, reach internationally, have a purposeful objective, and be unique in something.

DON'T EMPLOY SOMEONE YOU WOULD NOT LEAVE YOUR CHILDREN WITH

Seek out positive, uplifting, and action-oriented staff members. Ask them, "What exceptional people will you bring to the team?" Listen to their answer, as you want to look for leaders who will be thinking of onboarding more.

---

69 Richard Branson, "Richard Branson Quotes," BrainyQuote.com, https://www. brainyquote.com/quotes/richard_branson_452106.

THE ONLY WAY OUT OF THE RAT RACE IS TO TAKE RISKS

The first time I read that elderly people often regret not taking risks, it impacted me.[70] Working outside of your comfort zone is often necessary to get ahead in the long term and carry out your mission.

NO PLAN B

If you're considering a backup plan, you could be setting yourself up for potential failure because you're dividing your energy and attention between two plans. By removing the safety net of a plan B, we are forced to put all our effort, determination, and resources into making our plan A work. Don't obsess over short-term results, as projects take time and planting the seeds to enjoy later will be worthwhile.

BAILING WATER IN A LEAKY BOAT DIVERTS ENERGY FROM ROWING THE BOAT

Prioritize constant growth over optimizing the processes.

DON'T FALL IN LOVE WITH YOUR COMPANIES—THEY HAVE NO SOUL

All companies, like all people, will die sooner or later, so sell them whenever the appropriate moment arrives.

WHETHER YOU WORK FOR SOMEONE ELSE, OR YOU MANAGE A BUSINESS, ALWAYS BE YOUR OWN BOSS

Non ducor; duco (I am not lead; I lead). And if you work for others, ask for a fair amount of shares in the company or at least share options.

---

70   A. Pawlowski, "How to Live Life without Major Regrets: 8 Lessons from Older Americans," November 17, 2017, https://www.today.com/health/biggest-regrets-older-people-share-what-they-d-do-differently-t118918.

© Glasbergen/ glasbergen.com

GLASBERGEN

CHAPTER 7

LISTENING FOR STRONG COMMUNICATION

When my daughters travel with me, they are sometimes surprised at the conversations I have. Every time I get in an Uber, for instance, I ask the driver about their life and business. I want to see how they view the city or the country where we are, and their perspective on politics, too.

I do the same in other areas of my life. In the companies where I've worked, I always learn the names of everyone, including the cleaning crew and security teams. This, too, sometimes catches the attention of my family members. In one case, I remember running back to the office at night with my daughters to grab a document I needed. As we entered, everyone knew my name and greeted me. I, in turn, asked about their families and how they were doing.

Part of the reason for me doing this is because everyone is important, regardless of their role. In addition, for leaders, it is a crucial skill to be a strong communicator. This starts not with speaking, but with listening. It allows you to learn about others and build trust, empathy, and stronger relationships. In my experience, I've watched leaders—well, let's call them managers, which is a better explanation of them—who are clearly thinking of other things when someone is talking to them. Even if they are hearing what is said, they may not be processing it. Only when they rarely slow down and actively listen, they gain an understanding of the message or idea being shared. And while it's very understandable that leaders have many concerns and tasks to juggle and may struggle to focus, the ones that actively listen stand out from the rest. Those with charisma are often good listeners, as people feel good when they communicate with them. They listen intently and show that they value what is being shared with them.

One area that I like to emphasize when it comes to listening is to pay attention to oneself as well. Taking time for introspection is essential to be a good team player and leader. Ask yourself why you feel a certain way, or what happened that made you upset. Think about the words you want to say in an upcoming meeting, especially if you know there will be tension in it. Reading and listening to podcasts are other ways to listen on your own and grow internally. At work, listening to feedback can help you see blind spots you may not have been aware of. You can then correct your mistakes or behaviors to improve the situation.

I often make investment decisions based on listening well to absorb what is being said and analyze the information. As a child, I would read out loud to myself because of my dyslexia. This gave me a chance to confirm whether what I was reading was correct. In some cases, when I was reading, I would misidentify a word or letter, and then the noise that came out of my mouth would not sound right to my ear. I used this to self-correct my reading and improve it. It also helped me to train my patience and active listening skills.

These days, I put emphasis on listening and communication in work meetings, too. I have been known to run meetings with no phones allowed, so we can all focus on face-to-face time. In fact, I've also had team members using pencils and paper to take notes, so we can stay away from devices. One time, a worker pulled out his mobile at a meeting. To make my point, I took his device and threw it out the window. (I had a good relationship with him, and I got him a better phone after the meeting, but the action helped prove my point! No one ever pulled out a phone after that!)

Unfortunately, poor communications skills can lead to missed business opportunities. I think of a time when I went to a place to get a massage. I enjoyed the session, and I wanted to buy a package of sessions, but during the discussion with the dependent workers, I was interrupted again and again. I ended up not purchasing more sessions there, simply because I couldn't get a word in!

The following quotes are some of my favorite sayings and descriptions about communication. As you read through them, take some time to reflect on your daily conversations. You might learn strategies that you can use to help you improve your listening skills. I see this as an ongoing exercise. I find that some of my best ideas often come from unexpected conversations, so I stay open to all input, all the time. And I'm continually thinking about how I can be more aware of my surroundings to keep my relationships healthy and grow my businesses.

LEADERS AND COMMUNICATION
TO REACH YOUR FULL POTENTIAL, IMPROVE YOUR COMMUNICATION SKILLS

Most of today's relationship problems are caused by people's inability to communicate. Start by becoming more aware of how you speak and your body language. Next, acknowledge the worth of others by giving them your full attention when they speak. Finally, infuse every interaction with positive infectious energy.

TRUST IS NOT FORMED THROUGH A SCREEN, BUT ACROSS A TABLE

As a rule, get face-to-face meetings if possible. I'm also reminded of a quote by Brené Brown: "We need to trust to be vulnerable, and we need to be vulnerable to build trust."[71]

TREAT EVERYONE DECENTLY TO GET THE BEST OUT OF THEM

Always respect everyone. Understand everyone's strengths and weaknesses, and make the best of their strengths, always with kindness.

IN A PRESENTATION, COUNT THE LAUGHS

If you don't have fun, they won't either. The more laughs, the more probable you will sell.

IN EVERY PRESENTATION BECOME AN ACTOR ON A STAGE

Analyze, synthesize, rehearse, and perform to be worthy of applause. Avoid this funny comment about a very boring presentation that I heard: "We forgot the beginning, we didn't listen to what followed, and nothing pleased us as much as the end."

---

71   Brené Brown, "Brene Brown Quotes," Goodreads.com, https://www.goodreads.com/quotes/9836685-we-need-to-trust-to-be-vulnerable-and-we-need.

ASKING QUESTIONS IS MORE HELPFUL THAN OFFERING ADVICE

Try to phrase questions beginning with words like "What?" Stay away from those that start with "Why?"

IF YOU NOTICE A PROBLEM, DON'T PASS BY WITHOUT ADDRESSING IT

Either fix it yourself or ask someone else to look into it. This applies to your home, friends, and wider community.

EVERYONE HAS A DIFFERENT PERSPECTIVE

Focus on the positive or practical ones.

WHEN IN DOUBT, KEEP IT SHORT AND SWEET

As my great uncle Eugenio d'Ors said, "A synthesis is worth ten analyses."[72]

ASK INSTEAD OF COMPLAINING

To get what you want, improve your skills at requesting. The only thing worse than provoking difficult workplace discussions is not having difficult workplace discussions.

PLAN, PRACTICE, AND ROLE-PLAY BEFORE A TOUGH CONVERSATION

The impression you make is more important than your technical know-how.

---

72   Bernardo Peña, "Frases célebres de Eugenio d'Ors," PsicoActiva.com, May 18, 2023, https://www.psicoactiva.com/blog/frases-celebres-de-eugenio-dors/.

SUREFIRE SIGNS? ACT!

Watch for signals that indicate your boss or your partner is about to sit you down for a difficult discussion. They may no longer seek out your opinion. Previously long conversations could now end after a minute or two. They might not return your calls or respond to your emails. If you see these signs, do something to learn about the problem so you can take action to correct it.

BREAK THE ICE WITH FORS

Ask about their Family, Occupation, Recreation (hobbies), or Success (achieved or desired).

UTILIZE MASS COMMUNICATION

Make the most of synchronous communication such as lunches (try to never eat alone), meetings (keep them short to be productive), and video calls (to build rapport). Use asynchronous communication to keep the discussion going. Consider tools like Slack, Notion, Vidyard, and Discord for real-time updates and asynchronous collaboration.

YOUR LABELS BECOME SELF-FULFILLING PROPHECIES

If you put negative labels on your colleagues or kids, they will see themselves in a similar way. Instead, identify the positive points in other people, and use your words wisely to reinforce their positive behaviors.

DON'T SAY THANK YOU; DO THANK YOU

Practicing gratitude daily is critical to enhance your mental resilience. Like building muscle, cultivating gratitude requires consistent effort. Use your smartphone as a journal to record your daily reflections, such as what you feel grateful for and how you are going to pay forward. Or try my method: Rather than keep a journal, I use my three teeth brushing moments as my daily reflection and gratitude times. I also like to take a deep breath and laugh before every meeting to send good vibes to the people I will meet.

ACT, DO NOT EXPLAIN

You can often be more influential through your actions rather than your words.

WE DON'T KNOW WHAT WE DON'T KNOW

Just listen. Assume that the person you are with might know something you don't. Be open to new perspectives. Appreciate all ideas. Everyone knows more or has more experience than you in an area. As Charlie Munger used to say when analyzing investments, "Any year that passes in which you don't destroy one of your best loved ideas is a wasted year."[73]

WHEN NEGOTIATING, THE LESS YOU TALK THE BETTER

Firstly, the less you talk, the smarter you appear. Secondly, when you have already shared your positioning you have no place else to go but down by continuing to talk. Most of the time, the next person to talk usually loses. People hate silence, as it makes them uncomfortable, so they begin to talk and may share critical information that you could use during the negotiation in your favor.

---

73   Charlie Munger, "Charlie Munger Quotes," WonderfulQuote.com, https://www.
      wonderfulquote.com/a/charlie-munger-quotes.

WHEN ARGUING, TAKE A TIME-OUT TO GAIN CONTROL AND CALM DOWN

If possible, determine a specific goal for the confrontation before it occurs. Think about what you want to say and how to say it. Control your words and avoid raising your voice, interrupting, threatening, or laying out ultimatums.

PRAISE IN PUBLIC, CRITICIZE IN PRIVATE

Give credit where credit is due, and criticize the behavior, never the person. If you are the one criticized, evaluate what is said. Remember Marcus Aurelius's words, which indicate that if the criticism is correct and we are in error, then the person has done us a favor and we can correct our mistake.[74]

TAILOR YOUR PRAISE

Everyone has personal preferences. Some will love it if you applaud them during a staff meeting. Others will prefer you to say thank you in private. But do not lose any opportunity to provide genuine and well-deserved praise.

WHEN CRITICIZING, USE THE SANDWICH METHOD

Begin and end with some sincere compliments. And always make sure that the criticism is constructive.

USE IMPACTFUL WORDS AND PHRASES

The six most important words a leader can speak: "My confidence in you is total." The five most important words: "I am proud of you."

---

74 "How to Not Be Afraid of Criticism," Daily Stoic, https://dailystoic.com/how-to-not-be-afraid-of-criticism/#:~:text=As%20Marcus%20Aurelius%20writes%2C%20if,and%20already%20be%20fixing%20it.

The four most important: "What is your opinion?" The three: "If you please." The two: "Thank you." The most: "You."

LEARN PUBLIC SPEAKING TECHNIQUES

Join Toastmasters or a similar organization to learn about public speaking. Don't let stage fright rob you of your success; instead transmit the preperformance anxiety into fuel to enjoy the show. Additionally, remember that people dislike those who behave like know-it-alls and brag about their position or role. Try to make good use of jokes that involve a bit of self-criticism to release the tension in the room, or devise a hilarious interpretation of something familiar, such as a competitor's acronym. (I remember I laughed when I heard someone indicating that the name of Ford in reality meant Fix Or Repair Daily!)

MASTER THE ART OF STORYTELLING

Great speakers tell stories to express their passion for the subject and to connect with their audiences. Stories illustrate, illuminate, and inspire.

TELL A STORY WITH PASSION RATHER THAN RELATING A FACT

Inspire the audience instead of motivating them. Motivation lasts a moment, while inspiration stays for years. Finish big with a laugh, a tear, or a powerful statement. One big advantage of moving with purpose and passion is that difficulties don't arouse as much anxiety or stress.

SMARTER ALTERNATIVE INVESTMENTS

IT IS THE LEADER'S JOB TO INITIATE
CONTACT WITH PEOPLE

After starting the conversation, listen and don't interrupt. Avoid words such as "no," "but," and "however," which could have a negative connotation.

A SHEPHERD SHOULD SMELL LIKE HIS SHEEP

Do not lose touch with those who work for you. People are not interested in how much you know, but in how much you care about them. Ask about their lives outside of work, understand their families, and when things get rough, show up!

© Glasbergen/ glasbergen.com

"Success isn't as rewarding as it seems.
Caesar was the greatest emperor who ever
lived and they named a salad after him."

CHAPTER 8

THE KEYS TO LEADERSHIP

Great leadership begins with the basic principles of having a purpose, strong relationships, being open to opportunities, and actively listening. It also includes knowing how to build a team, delegate, and make decisions. The choices that leaders have to make are often difficult and have outcomes that affect employees.

For these reasons, leadership is a complex area and involves continual learning. I am always reading and gathering information on how to develop my own skill set. I have been in many leadership positions, starting with roles such as the chief business development officer of Codere Group, and CEO of Codere Interactiva. While there, I oversaw a tenfold increase in revenues and profits before its unicorn valuation IPO. I was also president of Intralot, a publicly listed gaming and lottery technology supplier and one of the largest sports betting operators in the world. I've served as vice president of global sales for FreeBalance, a Canadian consulting and SaaS company that has a mission to empower governments to drive economic growth and foster digital transformation. I'm GP of Savia Capital, an alternative investment fund, and chairman of Reental, the leading investment platform for real estate tokenization.

I mention these here because throughout my career, in every leadership position I've held, I've grown and developed teams to carry out the work. When hiring, I like to do more than ask several questions in an interview. I prefer to take candidates out to lunch, where the conversation can cover their family, interests, dreams, and hobbies. As I listen to them, I can learn what's important to them and see if their values align with the company's culture.

I also try to share expectations with new hires, which include a need for transparency and transmitting ideas in a constructive way. I strive for empathy among team members and believe mistakes should be allowed. In fact, we can use errors to learn and grow together. Still, I set some boundaries, and will mention that after three strikes (or similar mistakes), a person will usually be asked to leave. I prefer brief stand-up meetings, which allow everyone the chance to stretch and be to the point in their communications. After laying out these guidelines, I like to meet with a new hire after a month to check in with them.

I look for input before making decisions for the company, especially when they are about sensitive matters. At one of the multinational companies where I had a leadership role, I was part of a team that grew the company's workforce to thousands of employees. However, at one point, due to a change in circumstances, we had to let people go. It was an immense challenge, and it weighed heavily on my shoulders. I looked for ways to let people stay a little longer, or at least find a new direction or position. It was a very difficult time, and I found that presenting the news in an honest way, along with gathering insight from others, helped us all get through the challenge.

Being at the top isn't easy, and it can be useful to see the approach others have taken to successfully lead. In his book *Diary of a CEO,* Steven Bartlett, an entrepreneur and investor,[75] shares some of his own learnings from holding this position. I'm listing some here to get us started on this topic:

- The spiritual leader Yogi Bhajan once said: If you want to learn something, read about it. If you want to understand something, write about it. If you want to master something, teach it.

- If you don't care about tiny details, you'll produce bad work because good work is the culmination of hundreds of tiny details. The world's most successful people all sweat the small stuff.

- You can predict someone's success in any area of their life by observing how willing and capable they are at dealing with uncomfortable conversations. Your personal progression is trapped behind an uncomfortable conversation.

In your own areas of leadership, you'll have choices to make and people to collaborate with. I advise you to consider the following quotes as a learning experience. You may be able to find some ideas that you can apply to your own workplace. Even if you're not in a leadership role yet, knowing what to do (and what to avoid) can help you prepare for the road ahead.

---

75   Steven Bartlett, *The Diary of a CEO* (London: Ebury Edge, 2023).

ON LEADERSHIP

TAKE FULL RESPONSIBILITY FOR YOUR DECISIONS

Be accountable, reject your own victimization, and avoid negative people.

TO OPEN THE OTHER PERSON'S MIND TO YOUR ARGUMENT, TELL THE TRUTH—OR AT LEAST DON'T LIE

And be yourself. That's enough.

BE KIND, THANKFUL, AND COURAGEOUS

Even though it can be hard to be courageous, it's often necessary if you want to do what makes your heart sing. Sometimes, following your passion will lead to unexpected success.

LEADERSHIP IS NOT ABOUT DOING BUT ABOUT BEING

Or at least, leadership is about doing less and being more.

LEADERSHIP IS SITUATIONAL

The type of leadership (authoritarian, motivational, servant, etc.) to be applied in each moment will depend on the circumstances and people you are leading. Generally speaking, avoid the strict autocratic style and, on the other extreme, a permissive one that fulfills everyone's requests. For most occasions, try the authoritative style, which is supportive but not controlling. It is usually the most effective approach. Instead of asking, "Do you have any problem?" ask, "Is there anything you'd like me to help with?"

LEADERS MAKE THE RULES VERSUS PLAY BY THE RULES

Puppets just maintain the social status quo; leaders break ranks from time to time. The leader's job is not to tell the time but to build clocks that last and transcend generations. Leadership is about going where no one else has gone before.

THE TOP SKILL OF ANY LEADER OR CEO IS SELLING

The other two skills are listening and delegating. Mission-driven leaders have something to teach. Their top mission is to keep the vision alive so people can understand it and see their role in accomplishing it.

GOOD PEOPLE DO SOMETHING

It's not enough to avoid evil. It's also essential to look for ways to take action and help others.

BE A FORCE FOR GOOD

This includes the small stuff, too. If there's a piece of paper on the ground, bend over and pick it up. Be an example, and remember that there are not poor teams, but rather terrible leaders.

MANAGE BY INTERACTING WITH VALUES

Be a demanding boss who walks the talk.

HE WHO SHINES DOES NOT ILLUMINATE

Become a lighthouse, not a flashlight in the face. This can take time. As my Italian friends used to tell me about leadership, "*No si nasce, si diventa*" (You are not born, you become).

DON'T FAKE IT TILL YOU MAKE IT

"Fake it till you become it," according to Amy Cuddy. This quote was one of the main takeaways from the leadership best practices program I participated in at Harvard Business School.[76]

START WITH WHY

In his book *Start with Why*, Simon Sinek shows that leaders who have had the greatest impact on the world all think, act, and communicate in the same way. They start by explaining their "why." "People don't buy what you do; they buy why you do it," he says. However, the why must be accompanied and connected to the "how." There are many examples that illustrate this principle. Bill Gates had the idea for Microsoft, but Paul Allen built it. Steve Wozniak created Apple, but it was Steve Jobs who clarified the company's "why." One person may have the idea/vision (why), but someone else must have the capabilities/resources (how).[77]

LEADERS CANNOT KEEP A LOW PROFILE—
THEY NEED TO BE VISIBLE

The most successful leaders prepare and perform before meetings. They are generous and energetic, and they are constantly learning, networking, running smart risks, and taking action.

SHARE THE BAD NEWS AS SOON AS POSSIBLE

This creates trust in the long run.

---

76   Janel Ryan, "Fake It Till You Become It," Netscout.com, May 3, 2018, https://www.netscout.com/blog/fake-it-until-you-become-it-amy-cuddy.

77   Simon Sinek, *Start with Why* (London: Penguin, 2011).

DO NOT BLAME ANYONE

If you make accusations, it will break confidence. Also own your mistakes. Although no self-flagellation is needed, forgive when you or others slip up.

THE BUCK STOPS HERE

Take responsibility and don't delay the tough conversations or decisions.

BE WISE, BOLD, AND A GOOD TEAM PLAYER

Wisdom enables us to recognize when circumstances are shifting. We need to have the courage to seize those opportunities when they arise. It is also important to be a good team player. While you will often be the main player, you can never win big alone. According to Michael Jordan, "Talent wins games, but teamwork and intelligence win championships."[78]

ENGAGE IN TRIAL AND ERROR, FAIL, AND GET BACK TO IT

Michael Jordan also said, "I can accept failure, everyone fails at something. But I can't accept not trying."[79] Focus on incremental steps rather than dramatic moves. For example, try a trial period at a new job before you fully commit.

---

78 Michael Jordan, "Michael Jordan Quotes," BrainyQuote.com, https://www. brainyquote.com/quotes/michael_jordan_167383.

79 Michael Jordan, "Michael Jordan Quotes," BrainyQuote.com, https://www. brainyquote.com/quotes/michael_jordan_385092.

© Glasbergen/ glasbergen.com

"Things always get better after they get worse.
So it's good to make things worse as quickly as possible."

CHAPTER 9

THE UNIQUELY RESISTANT YOU

When I was growing up in Spain, there was a requirement to take a driving test to get a license. You had to be at least eighteen years old to be eligible for the exam. If you passed, you could legally drive, and if you failed, you would have to retake the test to get the license.

When I turned eighteen years old, I wasn't worried. I had already been driving since I was sixteen years old. I would take my father's car (while he was asleep) and go out with friends, and I never had problems behind the wheel. In fact, I loved it. I signed up for the test and assumed it would be easy.

To my surprise, the exam didn't go as I planned. I made a mistake and ended up failing the test. I had to go home that day without a license. Eventually I retook the test and passed, but the event was so unexpected that it sticks in my mind still today.

Not long after, I had to take another peculiar exam. This was a general one, and the results would either open the door to a university or lead you to look for something else. I wanted to go to a specific college, and I knew I had to pass the test with flying colors to get there.

At the time, students spent several months studying to get ready for the big day. It was a bit like trying to remember everything we had learned in the last five years. There were two main categories: sciences and the arts. On the day of the exam, a lottery would determine one of these, and it would be applied to the text. If science came up, we would have to answer questions that related to science and vice versa.

I decided to place a bet. I would study hard for the science category and take a chance that it would be the one chosen on the day of exams. That way, I could do very well and give thorough answers. I also saved myself from reviewing material that I wasn't as interested in.

The anticipated day arrived, and I watched, along with the other students, to see which category was selected. Similar to a game at an arcade, the individuals in charge drew out a ball. One of the balls would indicate the arts, while the other signaled for science. All eyes were on the instructors as they set up the lottery. Then they picked a ball, and it was for the arts.

An intense stress washed over me. I hadn't studied at all for that category. I had a choice of not answering any questions, or simply doing the best I could. I decided to give it a try.

I didn't get a high score as you can imagine. I did, however, secure the needed marks to enter the desired university. Once there, I double-majored in business and economics, two subjects I was passionate about, and since then I have tried to instill in my daughters the principle of lifelong learning and humility, which led me to continue my studies and obtain an MBA from IESE, a masters in finance from CEF, as well as numerous other programs at Harvard Business School, Stanford, MIT, and Berkeley, among others.

Perhaps you have had a moment (or more) when you feel like you have failed. Besides not passing my driver's test on the first attempt and not knowing as I wished the answers to the college entrance exam, I have faced many other setbacks. I've sat on boards and reached a point where I didn't see eye to eye with others involved in the company. I've been let go and have had to say goodbye to others, too.

Through it all, I've found different techniques and strategies to get through the hard times. If you're thinking outside the box, breaking some rules or the status quo to create a positive change, and trying to make a difference as an entrepreneur, failure will likely be part of that journey. It doesn't have to be an end point, though. Instead, it can be a moment that allows you to reflect, learn, and set up a plan to move forward.

In the following section, you'll have a chance to observe some of the phrases that have most helped me. I invite you to consider them for your personal and professional life, too. They can be used to evaluate risks, make decisions, and stay motivated. Once you get through the setbacks, you will be stronger and wiser to move ahead into better and more successful days.

OVERCOMING FAILURE AND BUILDING RESILIENCE

FAILURE IS NOT HAVING THE COURAGE TO TRY

In fact, there is no such thing as failure. Failure is an ego's terminology; our essence just learns and improves. As Winston Churchill said,

"Success is stumbling from one failure to another with no loss of enthusiasm."[80]

RECOGNIZE IT'S OK TO DO HARD THINGS

Ralph Waldo Emerson stated, "What you are afraid to do is a clear indication of the next thing you need to do."[81]

ACCEPT YOUR REALITY

Whether it is bad or good, keep going. A bad event or fortune can always be transformed into something of value, even if it is only to gain experience and the ability to sympathize with others in a similar situation. As my Latin teacher taught us: *Per aspera ad astra* (through hardships to the stars).

REMEMBER ANOTHER PLAN WILL COME ALONG

"Prepare for the worst and hope for the best but take solace in knowing you will be OK even if everything does go south," according to Trey Gowdy.[82]

THE MOTIVATION IS OVERVALUED AND THE WILLPOWER UNDERVALUED

There is an allegory about the length of the candle versus the match. The length of the candle represents willpower. The match represents

---

80   Winston Churchill, "Winston Churchill Quotes," Goodreads.com, https://www.goodreads.com/quotes/19742-success-is-stumbling-from-failure-to-failure-with-no-loss.

81   Ralph Waldo Emerson, "Ralph Waldo Emerson Quotes," Goodreads.com, https://www.goodreads.com/quotes/9989196-what-you-are-afraid-to-do-is-a-clear-indication.

82   Trey Gowdy, "Start, Stay or Leave Summary," Instaread, https://instaread.co/insights/self-help-personal-growth/start-stay-or-leave-book/26l8rq67d9.

motivation. To optimize your willpower, you will need to harness the power of the three statements that our prefrontal cortex controls. These are I will, I won't, and I want. Don't let one rule over the others. Rather, consider these three questions in equal parts.

NEGOTIATE WITH FEAR, PAIN, AND TIREDNESS

Listen and negotiate with them to take the next step and move to the next level of resilience. Pick yourself up and begin again because it doesn't end when you are tired but when you stop trying.

LIVE FACING YOUR FEARS

One at a time, and from little to bigger ones. When you conquer your fears you conquer your life. Remember Franklin D. Roosevelt's famous speech: "Nothing to fear but fear itself."[83]

THINK OF THE LONG TERM

As Napoleon Bonaparte shared, "The reason most people fail instead of succeed is that they trade what they want most for what they want at the moment."[84] And Winston Churchill said, "If you're going through hell, keep going."[85]

LIVING IN FEAR OF FAILURE WILL NEVER OFFER YOUR FULL POTENTIAL

People who are afraid of failure cannot step outside the box, much less think differently. Those who play it safe live life in lowercase letters

---

83 "FDR's Fireside Chat on the Recovery Program," Educator Resources, National Archives, https://www.archives.gov/education/lessons/fdr-fireside.

84 Napoleon Bonaparte, "Napoleon Bonaparte Quotes," Prisca Weems, https://www.priscaweems.com/.

85 Winston Churchill, "Winston Churchill Quotes," Goodreads.com, https://www.brainyquote.com/quotes/winston_churchill_103788.

and many regret it at the end of their lives. As General George Patton stated, "Fear kills more people than death."[86]

BEING COURAGEOUS IS NOT ABOUT HAVING NO FEAR, BUT ABOUT MOVING FORWARD WITH IT

Failure doesn't define you; it's your response that matters. As Winston Churchill famously said in a speech, "Success is not final; failure is not fatal: It is the courage to continue that counts."[87]

KEEP MOVING TOWARD YOUR GOALS

When everything seems to be going against you, remember that the airplane and the kite both take off against the wind, not with it. If you don't go after what you want, you will never have it. If you do not ask, the answer will always be no. If you do not move forward, you will always be in the same place. As Eleanor Roosevelt encouraged, "Do one thing every day that scares you."[88] She also stated, "You must do the thing you think you cannot do."[89]

MAINTAIN A TOUGH AND UPBEAT MINDSET

You are strong enough to face anything, even if it doesn't feel like it right now. All the water in the sea can't sink a ship unless it gets inside the ship. Similarly, the negativity of the world can't bring you down unless you allow it to come into you. Keep in mind that dreams

---

86 George Patton, "George S. Patton Quotes," Goodreads.com, https://www.goodreads. com/quotes/10213385-fear-kills-more-people-than-death.

87 Winston Churchill, "Winston S. Churchill Quotes," Goodreads.com, https://www. goodreads.com/quotes/3270-success-is-not-final-failure-is-not-fatal-it-is.

88 Eleanor Roosevelt, "Eleanor Roosevelt Quotes," Goodreads.com, https://www. goodreads.com/quotes/25106-do-one-thing-every-day-that-scares-you.

89 Eleanor Roosevelt, "Eleanor Roosevelt Quotes," Goodreads.com, https://www.goodreads.com/ quotes/3823-you-gain-strength-courage-and-confidence-by-every-experience-in.

do not come true at the snap of a finger. They require patience and determination.

DON'T BE INSPIRED; BE INSPIRATIONAL, BE BOLD

Be fearless, prepared, and ready. Seneca suggested, "Let us also produce some bold act of our own and join the ranks of the most emulated."[90] Ask for help, expect the best, plan for the worst, and be ready for a surprise. *Audentes fortuna iuvat* (fortune favors the bold).

WINNERS ARE NOT AFRAID OF LOSING

Losing is part of the path to becoming successful. Avoiding failure means avoiding success. Create a phoenix from the ashes! As Lao Tzu stated, "Failure is the foundation of success, and the means by which it is achieved."[91]

FAILURES ARE CHANCES TO LEARN AND MAKE IT BETTER THE NEXT TIME

Think about your biggest problem. Now, try to consider it a gift—an opportunity to learn something about yourself. Effective failure is an important learning and positive step toward success. It tells you what needs to be improved, so you don't have to fear it. Instead, you can listen to it. As Thomas Watson, founder of IBM, stated, "If you want to increase your success rate, double your failure rate."[92]

---

90   Seneca, "Moral Letters," Goodreads.com, https://www.goodreads.com/quotes/10286057-let-us-also-produce-some-bold-act-of-our-own-and.

91   Lao Tzu, "Lao Tzu Quotes," Goodreads.com, https://www.goodreads.com/quotes/9589293-failure-is-the-foundation-of-success-and-the-means-by.

92   Thomas Watson, "Thomas J. Watson Quotes," BrainyQuote.com, https://www.brainyquote.com/quotes/thomas_j_watson_209877.

KEEP YOUR HEAD UP

Famous movie star Charlie Chaplin said, "You'll never find a rainbow if you're looking down."[93] If you are at your lowest and see no way out, remember the sunshine always comes, even after a gloomy day.

MOST OF THE TIME, "NO" MEANS "I NEED MORE INFORMATION"

A "no" often means "I do not understand," "I need something different," or "I need to have details." So do not give up after a refusal, especially selling or negotiating, but interpret it as a need for further dialogue.

SUCCESSFUL PEOPLE FAIL FAR MORE OFTEN THAN UNSUCCESSFUL PEOPLE

It all comes down to their attitude toward obstacles. When a success-oriented person encounters an obstacle, they give it their best shot. And because some challenges are hard to overcome, they often fail. But they get up, dust themselves off, and try again.

YOU CAN'T LEARN TO RIDE A BICYCLE BY READING A BOOK

You learn to walk by walking. It is OK to read about the experiences of others, but nothing substitutes the learning from massive action. As my Asian friends used to remind me during my years of living in Indonesia and Singapore, once you carry your own water, you will learn the value of every drop.

---

93   Charlie Chaplin, "Charlie Chaplin Quotes," Goodreads.com, https://www.goodreads.com/quotes/77677-you-ll-never-find-a-rainbow-if-you-re-looking-down.

BE BRAVE

As Anaïs Nin shared, "Life shrinks or expands in proportion to one's courage."[94]

KNOW THAT IT WILL GET BETTER

As Saadi Shirazi stated, "Have patience. All things are difficult before they become easy."[95]

DIVE INTO DIFFICULT TASKS

As Erin van Vuren shared, "You are worn, cracked, and dented. And that is OK because I have never heard of a clean and shiny sword that won a war."[96]

DON'T LOOK FOR REASONS WHY
YOU CAN'T DO SOMETHING

According to George Washington Carver, "99 percent of all failures come from people who have a habit of making excuses."[97]

GROWTH AND COMFORT DO NOT COEXIST

Embracing failure and discomfort is the main vehicle for growth. The ultimate measure of us is not where we stand in moments of comfort, but where we stand at times of challenge. Peter McWilliams stated, "Be willing to be uncomfortable. Be comfortable being

---

94 Anaïs Nin, "Anaïs Nin Quotes," Goodreads.com https://www.goodreads.com/quotes/2061-life-shrinks-or-expands-in-proportion-to-one-s-courage.

95 Saadi Shirazi, "Saadi Shirazi Quotes," BrainyQuote.com, https://www.brainyquote.com/quotes/saadi_155337.

96 Susie Morgan, "Susie Morgan Blog," https://susiemorganlmft.com/worn-cracked-dented/.

97 George Washington Carver, "George Washington Carver Quotes," BrainyQuote.com, https://www.brainyquote.com/quotes/george_washington_carver_158549.

uncomfortable. It may get tough, but it's a small price to pay for living a dream."[98] And Miguel de Cervantes shared, "He who loses wealth loses much; he who loses a friend loses more; but he who loses his courage loses all."[99]

LIFE IS UNFAIR—GET USED TO IT

You will fail often; however, no matter how bad things get, you always have enough to keep going. And remember that every trauma, small or major, is an experience that can later be used to help others in similar situations. As Ernest Hemingway once wrote, "The world breaks everyone and afterward many are strong at the broken places."[100]

WAIT FOR THE SUN

If you're at your lowest and see no way out of it, just remember that after gloomy weather, we do see the sun again.

A NEW SEASON WILL COME

As the Japanese proverb states, "If you feel like you're losing everything, remember, trees lose their leaves every year, yet they still stand tall and wait for better days to come."

---

98 Peter McWilliams, "Peter McWilliams Quotes," BrainyQuote.com, https://www. brainyquote.com/quotes/peter_mcwilliams_393223.

99 Miguel de Cervantes, "Miguel Cervantes Quotes," Goodreads.com, https://www.brainyquote.com/quotes/miguel_de_cervantes_157065?__ cf_chl_tk=iwuKZjY5rgYuytBGU5mCD3_qQSmjRON0ayJO_0kD LPo-1711011938-0.0.1.1-1706.

100 Ernest Hemingway, "Ernest Hemingway Quotes," Goodreads.com, https://www.goodreads.com/ quotes/6592630-the-world-breaks-everyone-and-afterward-many-are-strong-at.

STRIVE FOR SMALL STEPS

Dalai Lama said, "The goal is not to be better than the other man, but your previous self."[101]

EMBRACE THE WISDOM OF THE KINTSUGI

Kintsugi is the Japanese art of repairing broken ceramic bowls. Sometimes a piece is more beautiful just because it is broken. Regarding ourselves, we can grow from our mistakes. For relationships, trust is like a vase; once it's broken, you can put it back together, but it's not the same. In a more positive approach, something similar happens with our mind: once stretched by a new idea, it never returns to its original dimensions.

LOOK FOR WHAT YOU CAN DO

According to Naval Ravikant, "Doctors won't make you healthy. Nutritionists won't make you slim. Teachers won't make you smart. Gurus won't make you calm. Mentors won't make you rich. Trainers won't make you fit. Ultimately, you have to take responsibility. Save yourself."[102]

ICHI GO ICHI E

This phrase, which seems to be an equivalent of the common phrase "carpe diem," was left to me in writing by a CEO of a Japanese company while we were sharing cups of green tea in Osaka. Let's live as if we were in an eternal tea ceremony, tasting every aroma, every flavor, the comfort and temperature of the environment, the good

---

101 Dalai Lama, "Dalai Lama Quotes," Goodreads.com, https://www.goodreads.com/quotes/658473-the-goal-is-not-to-be-better-than-the-other.

102 Naval Ravikant, "Save Yourself," MoveMeBlog, https://movemequotes.com/save-yourself/.

vibes of the people who accompany us, the conversation, and the laughter. (By the way, the other two interesting Japanese concepts I learned during my stay in Osaka were "Mushin" or "accept the constant change," and "Kintsugi" or the "art of resilience," which we practice in martial arts as training for life.)

WOBBLE YOUR WAY THROUGH TO SUCCESS

In doubt, the best thing you can do is the right thing. In fact, just doing the right thing is always enough. The worst thing you can do is nothing. As Theodore Roosevelt pointed out, "The only man who never makes a mistake is the man who never does anything."[103] J. K. Rowling shared, "It is impossible to live without failing at something, unless you live so cautiously that you might as well not have lived at all—in which case, you fail by default."[104]

KEEP YOUR CHIN UP AND CARRY ON

As Hanna Shebar reminded us, "You've made mistakes in the past, you will probably make more in the future. And that's OK."[105]

TAKE THE RIGHT APPROACH

According to Steven Bartlett, "Ninety-nine percent of the harm is caused in your head, by you and your thoughts. One percent of the harm is caused by reality, what actually happens and the outcome.

---

103 Theodore Roosevelt, "Theodore Roosevelt Quotes," BrainyQuote.com, https://www.brainyquote.com/quotes/theodore_roosevelt_163580.

104 J. K. Rowling, "J. K. Rowling Quotes," BrainyQuote.com, https://www.goodreads.com/quotes/61217-it-is-impossible-to-live-without-failing-at-something-unless.

105 "100 Best Quotes That Can Change Your Life," Thousif, https://thousif.org/100-best-quotes-that-can-change-your-life/.

Most of the time, the problem isn't the problem. The way you think about the problem is."[106]

REMEMBER TO KEEP CONTEXT

Rumi shared, "If everything around seems dark, look again, you may be the light."[107]

EXPERIENCE IS KING, CASH IS QUEEN

As H. Jackson Brown Jr. said, "I've learned that when a man with money meets a man with experience, the man with experience ends up with the money and the man with the money ends up with the experience."[108]

FAMILY WILL ALWAYS BE YOUR BIGGEST SUPPORTER

Family includes not only blood relatives but also support groups, mentors, or close friends. Through their support and encouragement, we can navigate the ups and downs of life, and receive guidance and wisdom when we face difficult decisions.

THE NORTH WIND MAKES THE VIKINGS

Just as northern storms make the Vikings the best sailors, most problems are opportunities to grow in work clothes. As sage Śantideva

106 Steven Bartlett, "Steven Bartlett," Twitter.com, https://twitter.com/StevenBartlett/status/1226192850104279040.

107 Rumi, "Rumi Quotes," Goodreads.com, https://www.goodreads.com/quotes/10574014-if-everything-around-seems-dark-look-again-you-may-be.

108 H. Jackson Brown Jr., "H. Jackson Brown Jr. Quotes," Goodreads.com, https://www.goodreads.com/quotes/7392015-i-ve-learned-that-when-a-man-with-money-meets-a.

said, "If the problem can be solved, why worry? If the problem cannot be solved, worrying will do you no good."[109]

THIS TOO SHALL PASS

In times of trouble, as well as in times of prosperity, we must always remember that everything will pass sooner or later.

WHAT DISTINGUISHES WINNERS FROM LOSERS IS THAT WINNERS TAKE ACTION AND NEVER GIVE UP

Baseball player Babe Ruth said, "It's hard to beat a person who never gives up."[110] My father, on one occasion when we were watching a boxing match together on TV, said to me, "Champions always get up after being knocked out." He was right.

109   Śantideva, "Śantideva Quotes," Goodreads.com, https://www.goodreads.
      com/author/quotes/29132._ntideva#:~:text=%C5%9A%C4%81ntideva%20
      Quotes&text=If%20the%20problem%20can%20be,will%20do%20you%20no%20
      good.&text=To%20cover%20the%20entire%20surface%20of%20the%20earth%3F.

110   Babe Ruth, "Babe Ruth Quotes," Goodreads.com, https://www.goodreads.com/
      quotes/5233279-it-s-hard-to-beat-a-person-who-never-gives-up.

© Glasbergen/ glasbergen.com

"For fast relief from stress, depression and anxiety,
four out of five doctors recommend money!"

SECRETS FOR SELF-ESTEEM

Whenever I think about building self-esteem, I'm reminded of the theory of the "10,000-hour rule." As noted by Malcom Gladwell in his book, *Outliers: The Story of Success,* if you work at something for ten thousand hours, you'll become an expert at it.[111] When I began to play chess, I learned that even more hours were needed to excel in it. About twenty thousand are required to become a master, and thirty thousand for a grand master.

With that in mind, it's critical to clarify that the area of self-esteem also requires many hours of dedication. As I look back on my own life and career, I've often jumped quickly from one role to another, or one experience to the next. I love to experiment, and that can reduce the chances of becoming an expert at something.

---

111   Nathan Colin Wong, "The 10,000-Hour Rule," National Library of Medicine, September–October 2015, https://www.ncbi.nlm.nih.gov/pmc/articles/PMC4662388/#:~:text=Throughout%20his%20book%2C%20Gladwell%20repeatedly,at%20least%2010%20000%20hours.

Still, in the area of self-esteem, it can be helpful to think about it as a long-term process that will develop. Once you've identified a skill you want to work on, you can set aside time to work on it, knowing that it won't change overnight. If you're doing something you enjoy, you could have fun with it and grow in confidence at the same time.

Part of having self-esteem includes an optimistic approach. We can control our mind and thoughts, and how you think internally can impact what happens on the outside. For this reason, I always emphasize that self-esteem starts from within yourself. As you build it up, you can celebrate your achievements, regardless of how small they are. Work to manage your negative thoughts, and in some cases a therapist or professional can help with this.

One of the ways I've found useful for building self-esteem involves aligning choices with principles and values. If you do this, you'll likely feel you're headed in the right direction. You can develop skills through your experiences and roles. This may make you open to new opportunities too, as you'll see them as a way to continue growing and fulfilling your purpose.

Pushing yourself out of your comfort zone and taking controlled risks can lead to positive self-esteem too. Just like when you're learning to ski, you might start with the blue slopes as soon as you dominate the green ones (meaning that you learned how to fall without hurting yourself ;)). They may make you uneasy at first, but over time, you'll master them. Then you can work your way up slowly to the black slopes. As you advance to each new level, it can be fun to see your skills improve.

And when things get tough, remember to push on. Navy SEAL David Goggins recommends the "40 percent rule," which means when you think you've given it your all, you still have about 60 percent left.[112] So carry on, and you may be surprised at what you can accomplish.

The path ahead will be far from perfect. In fact, mistakes will happen, and making them is often a sign that you are pushing yourself. Adam Grant, in his book *Hidden Potential*,[113] advises learning as much as possible to grow and asking others constantly for advice to set new goals based on what they suggest you work on next.

Finally, I always work to look at self-esteem as a very personal journey. I don't compare myself to others. Instead, I like to look back and reflect occasionally on how far I've come. The fun thing about life is that there are continual opportunities to work on improving, on creating an unbalanced harmony, and having a positive impact on others.

In the following quotes, you'll gain insight into building your own self-esteem. You might find some strategies that you can apply right away. As you do, keep in mind that change and development often take time, generally much more than we expect. Think about where you'll be in three or five years, or even longer. And then enjoy the journey.

---

112 Andrew Park, "Run for the Thrills: 5 Steps to Get You on the Road to Enjoying Running," Dobbins Air Reserve Base, November 3, 2017, https://www.dobbins.afrc.af.mil/News/Commentaries/Display/Article/1362718/run-for-the-thrills-5-steps-to-get-you-on-the-road-to-enjoying-running/.

113 Adam Grant, "What Straight-A Students Get Wrong," Oprah Daily, October 25, 2023, https://www.oprahdaily.com/life/health/a45600301/adam-grant-hidden-potential-book-excerpt/.

SELF-LOVE AND PERSONAL GROWTH

DON'T LET OTHER PEOPLE'S WORDS GET YOU DOWN

It is just a waste of time and energy. People cannot make you feel any negative emotion—anger, fear, sadness, oppression—unless you allow them. Forget about getting validation from others. Instead, take a step and keep going. Channel your energy into what makes you feel better.

SHIFT YOUR FOCUS TO A POINT OUTSIDE YOURSELF

Instead of seeking your value through things that are constantly in flux, like work or relationships, you can place God's eternal love at the center of your life. This will release you from the need to love yourself, so you can turn your attention to others.

WHAT HATERS THINK ABOUT YOU IS
NONE OF YOUR BUSINESS

Stop worrying about pleasing everyone. People's opinions are subjective and influenced by their own beliefs, experiences, and perceptions. They may form judgments based on limited information or biased perspectives.

EVERYONE HAS GOOD INTENTIONS

Living with this attitude is good for everyone. It can help you keep anger and resentment at bay. It's good for other people, too, because when you assume they're trying to be nice, you treat them with greater kindness, patience, and respect, and many times life surprises you with self-fulfilling prophecies and virtuous circles.

CHAPTER 10: SECRETS FOR SELF-ESTEEM

BE YOURSELF

According to André Gide, "It is better to be hated for what you are than to be loved for what you are not."[114]

ENJOY WHO YOU ARE TODAY

As Sigmund Freud stated, "One day, in retrospect, the years of struggle will strike you as the most beautiful."[115] And Rich Webster said, "Twenty years from now, you'd give anything to be: this exact age, this healthy, back in this exact moment. Take a second to enjoy it now."[116]

LOOK AT HOW FAR YOU'VE COME

Epicurus stated, "Do not spoil what you have by desiring what you have not; remember that what you now have was once among the things you only hoped for."[117] And Confucius added, "We have two lives, and the second begins when we realize we only have one."[118]

MAKE YOUR EGO POROUS

When we dissolve the boundaries of our ego, we become more open to new perspectives, experiences, and connections with others. It allows us to embrace empathy and understanding, leading to more meaningful interactions and relationships.

114 André Gide, "André Gide Quotes," Goodreads.com, https://www.goodreads.com/quotes/14304-it-is-better-to-be-hated-for-what-you-are.

115 Sigmond Freud, "Sigmond Freud Quotes," Goodreads.com, https://www.goodreads.com/quotes/33232-one-day-in-retrospect-the-years-of-struggle-will-strike.

116 Rich Webster, "Rich Webster Quotes," https://dailyquotes.io/page/2/.

117 Epicurus, "Epicurus Quotes," Goodreads.com, https://www.goodreads.com/quotes/169009-do-not-spoil-what-you-have-by-desiring-what-you.

118 Confucius, "Confucius Quotes," Goodreads.com, https://www.goodreads.com/quotes/950577-we-have-two-lives-and-the-second-begins-when-we.

BE SELF-CONTROLLED

As Pythagoras shared, "In anger, we should refrain both from speech and action."[119]

WRITE YOURSELF A LETTER

If you're struggling to speak to yourself with compassion after a setback, write yourself a message. Keep the tone gentle, as if you were talking to a close friend. Be compassionate and nonjudgmental in the message. Analyze what went wrong and how you can change things to feel happier and more fulfilled. Also, doing something called mirror work can change your state of mind, and even your life. Look into a mirror and speak words of affirmation back at yourself.

REFLECT ABOUT (AND IDEALLY WRITE DOWN) WHAT YOU ARE GRATEFUL FOR DAILY

Practice setting three phone alerts to go off during the day. When the chime sounds for the first and second alarms, pause for a moment and reflect on recent events you are grateful for. Think of how you will act and react during the next hours. At the last alert of the day, review what happened during the day, and celebrate the wins and learnings. It will improve your mood, establish happiness, and trigger positive emotions. Be aware of how much positivity you experience. And now that you are focused, take the opportunity to make a list of your goals with actionable small steps and begin to work on them (and remember that excuses are barriers between dreams and actions).

119　Pythagoras, "Quotes by Pythagoras," Goodreads.com, https://www.goodreads.com/author/quotes/203707.Pythagoras.

READ TO EXPAND YOUR MIND

As Patrick Bet David said, "Reading an hour a day is only 4 percent of your day. But that 4 percent will put you at the top of your field within ten years. Find the time."[120]

BE OBSERVANT OF EVERYONE

I am reminded of a time I was pushed during a school trip due to my smallness in stature. I was taken aback at the action and experienced the feeling of objectification. Since then, I have looked at people in a different way. Putting it in a positive light, the push made me realize that everyone we come across has something we don't. They may be physically stronger, or more knowledgeable in a certain area. Our experiences with others are a great opportunity to observe their knowledge or expertise.

PUT YOUR PROBLEMS IN PERSPECTIVE

Sometimes, even being stuck in a traffic jam can start to feel like the end of the world. But if you consider the obstacles you've encountered during your life, you'll realize that being caught up in traffic is the least of your worries. Create a list of the main setbacks you've had and keep the list at hand to remind you how resilient you are.

FOCUS ON GROWTH

When you focus on yourself, you'll grow. When you focus on negativity, negativity grows. As Steve Martin said, "Be so good that they can't ignore you."[121]

---

120 Patrick Bet-David, "Patrick Bet-David Quotes," Goodreads.com, https://www.goodreads.com/quotes/11667063-reading-an-hour-a-day-is-only-4-of-your.

121 Steve Martin, "Steve Martin Quotes," Goodreads.com, https://www.goodreads.com/quotes/541674-be-so-good-they-can-t-ignore-you.

BE HAPPY WITH BEING YOU

Steve Jobs shared, "Your time is limited so don't waste it living someone else's life."[122]

DON'T REPRESS YOUR EMOTIONS

This doesn't only apply to negative emotions. Positive feelings need to be expressed as well. Identify one or two people you can trust with your emotions (this could be a parent, sibling, friend, coach, or mentor) and actively share with them. Don't keep intense emotions—pleasant or unpleasant—to yourself. Once you let the emotions flow through you, you'll feel better. Additionally, the magic of pen and paper cannot be overstated. When you feel like no one is listening to you the way your feelings deserve without things getting messy, just pick up a pen and paper or your digital notepad to express your feelings. It works. And never stop looking up!

PUT YOUR HEART INTO PROJECTS

As Tony Robbins reminds us, "When we see technically perfect art, we like it. But when the artist gives their soul to art, we love it."[123]

BE A GO-GIVER, BUT ALSO A GO-GETTER

Being a go-giver means making a positive impact on others without expecting anything in return. Success should be measured by the positive influence and value we bring to the lives of others. Additionally, a go-getter possesses a driven, proactive, and entrepreneur-

---

122 Steve Jobs, "Steve Jobs Quotes," BrainyQuote.com, https://www.brainyquote.com/quotes/steve_jobs_416854.

123 Tony Robbins, *The Holy Grail of Investing* (New York: Simon & Schuster, 2024).

ial spirit. They are willing to put in the extra effort and dedication required to excel in their chosen field.

SELECT A CHALLENGING GOAL EVERY YEAR

This could be stretching every day, learning to play a new instrument, starting to practice a new martial art (I love karate, Krav Maga, and jujitsu, by the way). Or you could commit to reading more or making a frog call (a call you don't feel like doing) every week.

EMBRACE CHANGE

Avoid fretting about things you can't control. Never be afraid of taking controlled risks but be clever about which risks you take. It is not the strongest or the most intelligent who will survive and thrive, but those who can best manage change.

PLAY YOUR OWN GAME AND NEVER COMPARE YOURSELF WITH OTHERS

They probably started their career before you or have a different background. Just do the right thing to help everyone and avoid ego temptations to compete with anyone different from yourself. Compare yourself to you yesterday. Then try to be a better version of yourself every day!

LIFE HITS US ALL, AND SOMETIMES HARD; NO ONE IS SPARED

The difference is that some respond with less drama because they are already accustomed to increasingly unpleasant blows (you learn a lot about it in the dojo ;)). To build your resilience, try putting yourself in difficult situations from time to time. Try out ice baths, wake up early, or carry out intermittent fasting. Discipline will make you stronger.

IF YOU DON'T ASK, YOU WON'T GET IT

Always start conversations by showing concern about others. Create a conducive emotional environment by complimenting them if they deserve it or have earned it; help them if you can. However, you should also be able to communicate your own desires or ask for help if you need it.

KEEP AT IT

Never give up—just try to never make the same mistake twice. If you're feeling like you don't have direction, take some time to imagine receiving a terminal diagnosis. How would you change your lifestyle? What would you do or change if you had just a few days left in this life? As Paulo Coelho stated, "One day you will wake up and there won't be any more time to do things you've always wanted. Do it now."[124]

LIVE WITH AN "I CREATE MY LIFE" VERSUS A "LIFE HAPPENS TO ME" ATTITUDE

Take ownership and responsibility for your actions. Your life is the result of the lucky place where you were born, the choices others made for you early on, plus the many choices you can make today. You have control over your thoughts, attitudes, and behaviors, and these will significantly impact your outcomes.

Avoid living as a victim of circumstances, external forces, bad luck, or perceiving your qualities and circumstances as unchangeable.

---

124   Paulo Coelho, "Paulo Coelho Quotes," Goodreads.com, https://www.goodreads.com/quotes/594264-one-day-you-will-wake-up-there-won-t-be.

LOOK ON THE LIGHTER SIDE OF THINGS

"Don't take yourself too seriously. You're just a monkey with a plan," according to Naval Ravikant.[125]

UNHAPPY ONES EXPECT—WISE ONES ACCEPT

Expectations can sometimes lead to unhappiness. Acceptance is a wiser and more empowering approach to life. By practicing acceptance, we can find greater peace, contentment, and fulfillment. Rather than being held captive by unfulfilled expectations, we can choose to embrace life as it is and make the most of every moment.

FOCUS ON HEALING RATHER THAN INDULGING

Buying a new outfit or eating a cake won't make you feel better, but your brain tricks you into thinking it will. Instead, activities such as exercise, listening to music, massage, meditating, doing something creative, socializing with your friends or family, or reading are linked with the happy hormones in your brain, such as serotonin and oxytocin.

IT IS NOT THE CARDS WE ARE DEALT, BUT HOW WE PLAY WITH THEM

We can't control what occurs in life, but we can control our responses. What determines your fate is how you respond to an attack, rather than why you are attacked. By consciously choosing our responses and managing our emotions, we can cultivate a positive and proactive approach to life's ups and downs.

---

125 Naval Ravikant, "Naval Ravikant Quotes," Goodreads.com, https://www.goodreads. com/quotes/11107343-don-t-take-yourself-so-seriously-you-re-just-a-monkey-with.

IF YOU'RE NOT HUMBLE, LIFE WILL VISIT HUMBLENESS UPON YOU

Humility is a valuable quality that enriches our relationships and overall well-being. By embracing humility, we approach life with a mindset of continuous learning and gratitude. And remember that the ocean is the largest expanse of water because it is lower than all the rivers and swamps and remains open to all.

DON'T ACT LIKE SOMEONE ELSE; BE YOURSELF (UNLESS YOU ARE AN ASSHOLE)

Be an eagle; enjoy flying high. Remember, never compare yourself with anyone else—you are unique; there is no comparison. As Billy Graham said, "When wealth is lost, nothing is lost; when health is lost, something is lost; when character is lost, all is lost."[126]

MAKE YOURSELF PROUD, NO ONE ELSE

Create your personal board of advisors, including mentors, friends, and cheerleaders who share your enthusiasm and love you. Never take criticism from someone you would not take advice from.

---

126 Billy Graham, "Billy Graham Quotes," Goodreads.com, https://www.goodreads.com/quotes/653548-when-wealth-is-lost-nothing-is-lost-when-health-is.

© Glasbergen/ glasbergen.com

"I have a hard time finding a balance between work and work."

CHAPTER 11

FINDING HARMONY

If you look at my daily agenda, you'll see it is full of commitments, all identified by a color. I use colors to help me visually see how I am blocking out my time. For instance, one color might be used for business, another for family and friends, a different shade for leisure time, exercise, and so on. It helps me stay organized and quickly evaluate the way my hours are spent each day.

This is important for me, because I strive to maintain an unbalanced harmony between work and personal commitments (by "unbalanced harmony," I mean setting priorities on a weekly versus daily basis and being satisfied with putting urgent fires or needs first).

Sometimes I hear others say they are too busy and don't have time for certain activities. I like to respond with a strategy I have set up over the years. It involves setting priorities, and then using your time to carry them out. If I state that exercise is a priority, I might decide to have physical activity or at least stretching five days of the week. And then, I create two more time slots for exercise in my agenda. That way, if one of the first five times doesn't work, I have two more planned slots available that I can use.

As you think about unbalanced harmony, keep in mind that there will be periods in your life when more time will be spent on certain categories. You might have to dedicate a week to basically work, or travel to a conference, attend meetings and business-related dinners, and be away from your loved ones. Or you could have a week when you need to take more time to care for a family member or recover from a surgery. That said, you can always find ways to achieve that unbalanced harmony. You could take a couple of days off after a month full of work activities and travel. Or you might use a weekend to catch up on exercising and reading if you weren't able to fit it in during the week.

I also regularly evaluate my priorities and goals. I typically do this during the summer holiday, and around the new year. It gives me a chance to reflect on how I have used my time, and what I want to eliminate or add to my agenda. I might decide to spend more time learning about a different culture or country I haven't visited, so that will get included in the schedule for the coming months. I also look for toxic habits and relationships that should be reduced or removed.

I've found that maintaining some regular structure can also be helpful for such unbalanced harmony. For instance, I like to start the day with my meditation and reading, and also schedule time during the week for exercise and a massage. After work, I set aside my phone when it's time for dinner with my loved ones. When I'm with my family, we'll talk as we prepare the meal together. We'll share concerns, good news, and highlights from the day. We'll also listen to each other so we can pick up on ways to solve an issue or improve in a certain area where we are struggling. After dinner we might watch a movie or a series, ideally based on real events, though we are careful to get up after one episode or the determined time, usually forty-five minutes (movies are usually watched as a series of two or three episodes). We then go on to read and relax before going to bed.

Your agenda might look different, based on your priorities and personal life. I encourage you to think about how it's working for you, and if there are areas you'd like to change, always starting small to achieve stickiness. If you want to exercise more, try committing to two or three times a week, rather than five right away. You can build on the steps and gain momentum.

As you read the following quotes and sayings, consider how they might be applicable to your own life. You might find that you can better manage the hours in your days and weeks to create the unbalanced harmony you've been looking for.

PRODUCTIVITY AND LEISURE

MAKE YOUR BED EVERY DAY TO START WITH A COMPLETED TASK

Pave the road with small accomplishments. Small and simple tasks will make you more disciplined and capable.

PLAN YOUR LEISURE TIME TO INCREASE ITS VALUE

Treat your leisure time with the same importance as your work or other commitments. Having a routine or schedule will ensure that you make time for leisure regularly and will allow you to prepare.

FOLLOW ROUTINES

If you seek financial freedom, you must practice persistent financial discipline daily. To optimize your productivity, a rigorously disciplined approach to time management is critical.

SET MINI DEADLINES

Break big challenges or projects down into small, manageable steps and targets. Fight procrastination with mini deadlines that hold you accountable and split tasks up into more manageable chunks. Reward yourself whenever you meet the deadlines (the award is always in proportion to the achievement ;)).

GO AGAINST THE GRAIN

Rather than accumulating things, as society often advises, try to remove them. Reduce what you have to simplify your life.

THE SOONER YOU PLANT THE SEED, THE SOONER YOUR TREE WILL MATURE

The more you feed and water the tree, by saving and investing, the sooner you'll bask in contentment beneath its shade.

THE FASTER YOU RUN ON THE HAMSTER WHEEL, THE FASTER IT WILL SPIN

The hamster wheel symbolizes a cycle of constant motion and effort without necessarily making significant progress or finding fulfillment. Ensure that your actions align with your true goals and values rather than being driven solely by external pressures or a constant need for achievement.

A SEED NOT SOWN PRODUCES NOTHING

We reap what we sow. Beware of the excessive use of screens that is transforming *Homo sapiens* into *Homo videns*, undereducated by too many images and entertainment. On the contrary, read one extra page or practice that new language ten minutes longer than expected. Remember the saying, "Go the extra mile. It is never crowded."[127]

IF IT TAKES LESS THAN TWO MINUTES, DO IT; IF MORE, DELEGATE OR DEFER

Never do anything that someone else can do better, as well or at least at 80 percent of your capacity. As John Maxwell said, "If you want to do a few small things right, do them yourself. If you want to do great things and make a big impact, learn to delegate."[128]

WHEN FOLLOWING UP, KEEP BUSINESS CALLS TO A MAXIMUM OF FIFTEEN MINUTES

Short, friendly, and succinct calls make people eager to hear from you and look forward to your next call.

BEWARE OF PARKINSON'S LAW

This law states that work expands to fill the time available for its completion. By setting deadlines and limiting the amount of time you spend on each task, you will increase your efficiency, productivity, and leisure time!

PROCRASTINATION MAKES TOMORROW'S SLOPE STEEPER

Taking the easy route today leads to a more difficult time tomorrow. We economists use a theory called "delay discounting," meaning that if you need to wait for a reward, its value decreases. You can use it

---

127   Anonymous, "Anonymous Quotes," Goodreads.com, https://www.goodreads.com/quotes/7402341-go-the-extra-mile-it-s-never-crowded.

128   John Maxwell, "John Maxwell Quotes," Goodreads.com, https://www.goodreads.com/quotes/3216300-if-you-want-to-do-a-few-small-things-right.

to fight procrastination. Each time you are thinking about postponing something, pause for five minutes. By intentionally pausing (you cannot do anything during those five minutes), you are delaying the reward of doing something more fun than your initial obligation, and consequently it will feel less valuable. If you are wise, you will use that pause to reconsider the unpleasant consequences of postponing it until tomorrow, and you will get on to complete it right away.

SET PRIORITIES

List your top three priority tasks daily and build your schedule around them.

MULTITASKING DOES NOT INCREASE PRODUCTIVITY

Contrary to popular belief, multitasking is a trap and does not increase productivity. In fact, research shows two surprising facts about multitasking: First, it reduces productivity by as much as 40 percent. Second, those who multitask are typically the least able to do so successfully.[129]

SMART NETWORKING VERSUS LOW-QUALITY CONNECTING

Instead of blindly saying "yes" to every request for connecting, build the relationships that matter most. Replace large networks that often have little substance with smaller networks of connections that truly bring value or joy.

---

129 Emma Parsons, "Stop Multitasking, It Reduces Productivity by up to 40%," LinkedIn, March 7, 2021, https://www.linkedin.com/pulse/stop-multitasking-reduces-productivity-up-40-learn-3-time-parsons.

LOOK TO THE OUTDOORS

Allocate some "nature time" into your weekly schedule.

ATTEND ONLY SMART MEETINGS, IDEALLY WITH THE OPTIMAL SIZE

Do your best to get out of meetings that aren't necessary. If you do attend a smart meeting (those that are relevant to your work), exude positive energy, come prepared, listen, speak up (if you have value-added information to share), and avoid blaming others or self-promotion.

When it comes to optimal size, Amazon CEO Jeff Bezos lives by the "two-pizza rule"—no team should be so large that it needs to be fed with more than two pizzas. Research backs up Bezos's rule of thumb. Studies show that the optimal size for most teams to generate ideas or make decisions is four to six people.[130]

HEALTH AND WELLNESS

WE ARE IN CHARGE OF OUR OWN WELLNESS

A healthy lifestyle includes what and when you eat, when and how much you sleep, and when and how often you move. As Mahatma Gandhi once said, "It is health that is the real wealth and not pieces of gold and silver."[131]

---

130   "Two Pizza Teams," AWS Whitepaper, https://docs.aws.amazon.com/whitepapers/latest/introduction-devops-aws/two-pizza-teams.html.

131   Mahatma Gandhi, "Mahatma Gandhi Quotes," BrainyQuote.com, https://www.brainyquote.com/quotes/mahatma_gandhi_109078.

AVOID MENTAL LAZINESS AND LETHARGY

Read, do more mental calculations, and have more social relationships. Minimize the use of social networks and TV.

CHALLENGE YOUR BODY

Experiment with sports until you find one that fits your schedule and liking. Regular exercising makes your body more resilient. Always find time to take a walk at the very least. Create breaks to get out of your desk and stretch every ninety minutes. Since your body includes your brain, challenge it by practicing things you usually don't do to help new brain areas develop, or go for regular phone-free walks, ideally by nature, to let your brain wander and form new neural connections.

HAVE A PLAN A, B, AND C

Create a habit, such as going to the gym, running, or playing a new instrument. Identify days and times to do this as your plan A. Have a plan B if something expected comes up, and a plan C if you can't carry out either. It is not will, it is organization.

LISTEN TO HUNGER SIGNALS

Eat when you're hungry and get up even when you continue to feel a little bit hungry. This is one of the keys to staying fit and healthy. I have found that it is taught infrequently—especially in the West. Beware of overeating, especially before going to bed. When you overeat, your body's temperature will be too high to fall asleep comfortably.

CHOOSE PLANTS OVER PROCESSED FOOD

The rise of processed, unhealthy food makes us consume too many calories that are not filled with nutrients. A plant-based diet is low in fat and sugar, and rich in whole grains, legumes, fruit, and vegetables. It contains all the nutrients our bodies need.

BRUSH YOUR TEETH WITH YOUR NONDOMINANT HAND

It is not only a good brain training exercise, but it can also lead to better oral hygiene since you reach parts of your mouth that you would have missed with your regular routine. It's a win-win!

UNDER PRESSURE? PAUSE AND TAKE
THREE DEEP BREATHS

Instead of giving power to our elephant (the emotional part of our brain), inhale deeply, hold that breath, exhale slowly, and pause. It is also helpful to forget your worries for a moment.

IF YOUR MINDSET IS NOT ASSISTING, CHANGE IT

Use your challenges to develop a resilient mindset. It will help you to have the dexterity and clarity needed to face the darkest moments.

SUPPLEMENT DAILY

Try a multivitamin or antioxidant, omega-3 fish oil, probiotic, high-protein meal replacement, and vitamin D if it is a sunlight-challenged week.

EXERCISE YOUR BODY, MIND, AND SPIRIT

Give it all; when your body cannot continue, activate the energy reserve of your mind, and when you are mentally exhausted, pull on the reserve of your spirit.

GO TO SLEEP EARLY

Make time to rest, reflect, and restore yourself. Sleep is linked to your metabolism and contributes to insulin resistance. It boosts the mental cleaning service known as the brain lymphatic system. Research shows that sleep deprivation has similar effects on the body as chronic stress. Poor sleep makes you stressed, raising cortisol levels and blood pressure.[132]

SET A BEDTIME ROUTINE

Create a routine, such as a warm bath to start. Not only will you feel relaxed, but your body temperature will also drop, which signals the brain that it's time to sleep. Ensure your room is dark. Consider finding the sound of the sea, forest, or rain on YouTube or another app and turn it on as a trigger when you feel stressed or need to go to sleep.

SOMETIMES IT IS OK TO DO NOTHING

The Nietzsche phrase comes to mind: "He who fights with monsters should look to it that he himself does not become a monster ... when you gaze long into the abyss the abyss also gazes into you."[133] Occasionally, dedicating some time to thinking or resting is the best solution. Always in moderation, though. (God rested on the seventh day, not on the sixth *and* seventh.)

MODERATION IS CRITICAL, EVEN IF IT IS BORING

Unfortunately, you do not know what is enough until you discover what is more than enough.

---

132 "Good Sleep for Good Health," NIH, April 2021, https://newsinhealth.nih. gov/2021/04/good-sleep-good-health.

133 Friedrich Nietzsche, "Friedrich Nietzsche Quotes," Goodreads.com, https://www. goodreads.com/quotes/527253-he-who-fights-with-monsters-should-look-to-it-that.

GO BAREFOOT WHENEVER POSSIBLE

Especially if you can enjoy the contact with the grass or sand of the beach. This practice is often referred to as grounding or earthing, since it strengthens foot muscles, has a calming effect on the nervous system, and stimulates reflexology points. It can help improve proprioception (awareness of body positioning) and promote overall well-being by allowing electrons from the earth to enter the body and neutralize free radicals.

IT'S NOT SELFISH TO CUT TOXIC
PEOPLE OUT OF YOUR LIFE

Taking care of your emotional well-being is essential for leading a fulfilling life. Cutting ties with toxic individuals is an act of self-preservation and mental health.

ADD PROTEIN TO YOUR BREAKFAST!

Ensure that your breakfast (and of course, lunch and dinner, too) has protein in it. And reduce or eliminate starchy and sugary foods. It is also a good and healthy habit to add electrolytes to your water bottle.

DO YOUR BRAIN TRAINING DAILY

Exercise your brain by reading, doing math, learning a foreign language, or playing a new musical instrument. Have good social connections, play card games, or try out an online brain game. To take additional care of your brain, eat a Mediterranean style diet, because it is rich in antioxidants, healthy fats, omega-3 fatty acids, and brain-boosting nutrients such as vitamin E, vitamin B6, and folate. It also has minerals such as magnesium and zinc (these nutrients support various aspects of brain health, including memory, cognition, and mood regulation).[134]

PAUSE AND PLAN (RATHER THAN FIGHT OR FLIGHT)

Even though we don't have to run away from big-toothed predators these days, we do have other kinds of threats such as tempting donuts or cheesecakes. Just pause and plan, that is, take a moment to see if the food will be your weekly cheat meal. Having an occasional treat is fine but monitor your stress and dopamine triggers and avoid recurrent slippery slopes.

FEED YOUR HAPPY HORMONES

Reading, listening to music, meditating, exercising, receiving a massage, and socializing with friends and family are all linked with the happy hormones of your brain, such as serotonin and oxytocin. Consider one of these activities before the most common ways people deal with stress: eating, drinking, shopping, watching TV, or scrolling social networks.

ANTICIPATE POTENTIAL EMERGENCY SITUATIONS PRACTICING THE PACE PLAN

Through Krav Maga training with bodyguards, marshals, Navy SEALs, and members of the army, I learned that in the military they practice the PACE (Primary, Alternate, Contingency, Emergency) plan. It consists of practicing drills that identify the first choice for escape or primary plan, an alternate option if the first one is not possible, a contingency plan, and an emergency plan or last resort, where the goal is survival and injury will be considered preferable to mortal threats.

---

134 "Diet Review: Mediterranean Diet," Harvard T. H. Chan, https://www.hsph.harvard. edu/nutritionsource/healthy-weight/diet-reviews/mediterranean-diet/.

WRITE THEM A LETTER

If you are experiencing a loss, allow yourself to express strong emotions, such as sadness, to reduce its intensity. Remember that grief is an emotionally difficult period that can require psychological support. And sometimes, as I did after my father's passing, it helps to write letters to those who are no longer with us to say everything you did not have time to say.

MOTIVATION IS NOT A MYSTICAL FORCE BUT A LEARNABLE AND TRAINABLE SKILL

My key "aha" moment was understanding that motivation follows your actions, it doesn't precede them. When you are down, do something simple, no matter how small the action. Our relationship with setbacks is also crucial to maintaining motivation. The point is not to avoid missteps, but to learn to bounce back, seeing failure as a mentor rather than a punishment. Treat yourself to a setback with the same empathy and understanding as someone you love to regain motivation and stay on track!

WRITE YOURSELF A LETTER AS A REMINDER OF WHY YOU WANT TO CHANGE

There will inevitably be times when your motivation wanes. To remind yourself of how important it is for you to change, write a letter including why you've adopted this new approach to change. Then put the letter in a place where you'll remember to read it the next time you're feeling unmotivated.

THE SECRET OF HAPPINESS IS FREEDOM;
THE SECRET OF FREEDOM IS COURAGE

This journey toward freedom and happiness involves stepping out of our comfort zones and facing uncertainties. You may be going through hard times and perhaps the road ahead doesn't look easy. The secret to being brave and getting through is to constantly remind yourself of how lucky you have been and how lucky you are to be able to set yourself new and worthwhile challenges.

KEEP GOING

After getting thrown by an older, stronger kid, I looked for ways to defend myself. This led me to learn martial arts like karate, wushu, sanda, jujitsu, and Krav Maga. Since then, no one has ever laid a finger on me again—and not because they haven't tried—so there is always a silver lining!

YOUR LIFE IS 100 PERCENT YOUR OWN RESPONSIBILITY

It is not on them—it is on you. When things go south, and they will, beware of identifying yourself as a victim, blaming someone else, or hoping to get rescued by your boss, partner, or the government. You can become the survivor or hero of your own life, welcome new challenges, and embrace any opportunity for growth. Keep your accountability and motivation up by knowing what fulfillment means to you, being patient, pivoting as much as you need to, and enjoying what life brings you.

PICK UP YOUR JOURNAL AND DESCRIBE IN
DETAIL THE AUTHENTIC LIFE YOU DESIRE

What would you do or change about what you are doing presently to get you there? Do your beliefs, thoughts, and actions align with the authentic life you dream about? If they don't, what are you going to do about it? Write out how you will transit from your present life to the authentic one you deserve.

IN THE WOUNDS THE LIGHT APPEARS

The "wound" represents our vulnerabilities, struggles, and pain—both physical and emotional—that we experience throughout life. The light symbolizes wisdom, insight, and transformation. Our most profound moments of growth often arise from the very places where we have been hurt. As the Shōyō Rōku says, "On the withered tree, a flower blooms."[135]

CHANGE THE ROOTS TO CHANGE THE FRUITS

The "fruits" represent the visible results, circumstances, or experiences that we encounter in various aspects of our lives, such as relationships, career, health, or overall well-being. These outcomes are influenced by the "roots," which symbolize the underlying factors, beliefs, habits, or mindset that shape our actions and decisions. Most of the time, the only way to change others is to change ourselves first. Once we change our patterns, we'll find that other people are different, too.

IF YOUR OUTER LIFE ISN'T GOING WELL, REVIEW YOUR INNER LIFE

By nurturing our emotional well-being and overall mental health, meditating, exercising, and socializing, we are better equipped to face external challenges. Also, environmental factors can have just as big

---

135 "On the Withered Tree, a Flower Blooms," Buddha and the Big C, January 9, 2011, https://buddhaandthebigc.blogspot.com/2011/01/on-withered-tree-flower-blooms. html.

an impact as genes. For example, people are more likely to take risks after eating spicy food or listening to loud music.[136]

NEVER STOP PLAYING

In the words of George Bernard Shaw, "We don't stop playing because we grow old; we grow old because we stop playing."[137] I also love Sir Richard Branson's life philosophy: "I don't think of work as work and play as play. It's all living."[138]

SEEK THE COUNSEL OF AT LEAST THREE PEOPLE OLDER AND WISER

Go beyond your friends and parents and listen to others who are older, such as grandparents, or anyone who has extensive experience in any field.

MAKE SPREADING CONTAGIOUS ENTHUSIASM YOUR PERSONAL MOTTO AND LIVE IT!

Send a card or a message to someone thanking them or saying how much you appreciate what the person does. For example, our neighbor Joan sends us thank-you cards every time we help her (most of us just respond with a smile and a heartfelt thank you).

---

136 Diane Mapes, "Your Love of Spicy Foods Means You're a Risk-Taker," NBC News, August 6, 2013, https://www.nbcnews.com/healthmain/your-love-spicy-foods-means-youre-risk-taker-new-study-6c10851877.

137 George Bernard Shaw, "George Bernard Shaw Quotes," BrainyQuote.com, https://www.brainyquote.com/quotes/george_bernard_shaw_120971.

138 Richard Branson, "Richard Branson Quotes," Quote-Fancy, https://quotefancy.com/quote/757256/Richard-Branson-I-don-t-think-of-work-as-work-and-play-as-play-It-s-all-living.

BE OPEN TO NEW EXPERIENCES IN YOUR LIFE

It is never too late to learn a new thing. Whatever is flexible and fluid tends to grow, while whatever is rigid and stagnant tends to atrophy and die. In Bruce Lee's words, "The less effort, the faster and more powerful you will be."[139]

IF TIRED OR WORRIED, USE ONE OF
OUR WESTERN MANTRAS

I love simple three-word phrases such as just do it, let it be, it shall pass. If you don't feel like doing the goal for the day, like going for a run, start. Don't waste time thinking about how difficult the goal is or how tired you are; just go and do it.

Crush negative thoughts and replace them with good ones. Be aware of what you think about and consciously meditate on the positive. For example, instead of thinking that a goal is challenging, replace it with, "I can do this." Or use my wife's motto: "I am powerful, I can do anything," which is much catchier in Spanish because of its rhyme, "Soy poderosa, puedo con cualquier cosa."

KEEP THE POSITIVE FEEDBACK HANDY

Life is a lonely business, often filled with discouragement and rejection. Keep all positive feedback in a separate file; read it to boost your morale when you're feeling low.

Think about the benefits: Keep your mind focused on the impact that the goal you want to achieve will have on your life. This thought process will prevent you from dwelling on the negative. Find like-minded friends: Look for people with similar goals and work with them. These friends will increase your motivation.

---

139 Bruce Lee, "Bruce Lee Quotes," BrainyQuote.com, https://www.brainyquote.com/quotes/bruce_lee_110197.

WHILE THERE IS HOPE, THERE IS A WAY

Life is full of trials and tribulations, but blaming the circumstances or humiliating ourselves will make the days burdensome and tiring. Change will only occur if you are willing to take risks, and taking a risk does not have to be something big and drastic. Remember something that broke you in the past, then identify what helped you overcome your mindset and how it made you stronger!

LOOK FOR EXTENDING YOUR HEALTH
SPAN MORE THAN YOUR LIFE SPAN

The leading causes of death, which include cardiovascular disease, cancer, and neurological diseases, can be delayed by years with exercise and preventative measures.[140] The good news is that it's never too late to start and increase our life span and, more importantly, our health span. Plus, seniors lose muscle at a higher rate, so exercising earlier is an investment in such health span.

MEDITATION AND SELF-AWARENESS

MEDITATE BEFORE BREAKFAST AND DINNER

It will give you time to set your daily priorities and reflect about the day.

MEDITATION PRACTICE IS JUST ABOUT SITTING
AND REALIZING THAT ONE IS NO-SELF

Although meditation is a personal practice, the way to strengthen the spirit is through diligence. Get used to being at home in the muddy water. There is no better moment than this. Pray to God and listen

---

140 Saloni Dattani, Fiona Spooner, Hannah Ritchie, and Max Roser, "Causes of Death," Our World in Data, https://ourworldindata.org/causes-of-death.

to Him. From time to time, just surrender, focus on one thing until your thoughts start to wander, and then focus on your breathing to pull them back.

SIMPLY SIT

One of the most important things to do is daily sitting. And when I say sitting, I mean sitting comfortably but straight. (I read in a book that sensei Jon Kaban-Zinn used to say that the state of mind we achieve when we just sit in the right posture is itself enlightenment.) Finding twenty minutes twice a day can be a challenge (it's OK to begin with just five or ten minutes at first and gradually increase the time), but there's a reason some of the world's most successful and busiest people have made a habit of sitting and collecting their thoughts. It's worth the time.

MEDITATE—IT HELPS YOU STAY YOUNG!

Meditating has antiaging effects, since it increases your levels of telomerase, the enzyme associated with slowing the aging of cells.[141] Overall, an active waking day leads to a good night's sleep, which facilitates emotional health. Additionally, your psyche is a serious matter linked to your physical health. Unaddressed mental issues can lead to physical symptoms and high cortisol levels.[142] If you don't deal with negative thoughts, they will become negative actions that affect your well-being. So, don't be afraid to seek professional help if you need it.

---

141   James Kingsland, "Could Meditation Really Help Slow the Aging Process?" The Guardian, March 3, 2016, https://www.theguardian.com/science/blog/2016/mar/03/could-meditation-really-help-slow-the-ageing-process.

142   "Physical Health and Mental Health," Mental Health Foundation, https://www.mentalhealth.org.uk/explore-mental-health/a-z-topics/physical-health-and-mental-health.

THERE ARE NO FREE LUNCHES

We must pay the price of freedom. We must earn it, with steady, unrelenting practice. Only a Buddha has no resistance, and among the human population there are no Buddhas.

GO SHINRIN-YOKU

The Japanese practice of shinrin-yoku, or forest bathing, has antistress and antiaging effects. It increases the levels of telomerase, an enzyme associated with slowing the aging of cells.[143]

HAPPINESS IS TURNED ON FROM WITHIN

Your happiness today will depend on your current thoughts, decisions, and actions. Be especially conscious of them and know that you can tame them to be positive.

GROW WITH THEM

Learn from those who do good with love as well as from those who do bad with fear.

EMPATHIZING DOESN'T REQUIRE AGREEING

Show empathy to people acknowledging their pain, sharing how you feel. Understand them with kindness even if you disagree.

---

143 Bun Jin Park, Yuko Tsunetsugu, Tamami Kasetani, Takahide Kagawa, and Yoshifumi Miyazaki, "The Physiological Effects of Shinrin-yoku (Taking in the Forest Atmosphere or Forest Bathing): Evidence from Field Experiments in 24 Forests across Japan," *Environmental Health and Preventative Medicine* 15, no 1 (2010): 18–26, https://environhealthprevmed.biomedcentral.com/articles/10.1007/s12199-009-0086-9.

TAKE HOLD OF YOUR BREATH

Respond carefully to events. Live your life rather than letting your life live you. Smile at a stranger or at yourself in the mirror.

LOSE YOURSELF IN THE SERVICE OF OTHERS

As Mahatma Gandhi stated, it is the best way to find yourself.[144]

YOU ARE YOUR BEST HELPER

Many horse trainers beat horses for being untamable; it would be more appropriate to focus first on themselves and tame their mind first. Tame your mind, tame your ego.

CALM YOUR MIND WITH DEEP BREATHING

Stress will come and go in your life. You cannot always control whether stress happens or not, but you can decide how to handle it. Use deep breathing to relax and to pull your awareness back to the present. You can't stop the waves, but you can learn to surf.

LIFE FAVORS THE PREPARED MIND

You must be very selective about what you put into the lush garden of your mind.

PROTECT YOUR PEACE OF MIND

As Epictetus recommended, "Keep constant guard over your perceptions, for it is no small thing you are protecting, but your respect,

144 Mahatma Gandhi, "Mahatma Gandhi Quotes," BrainyQuote.com, https://www. brainyquote.com/quotes/mahatma_gandhi_150725.

trustworthiness and steadiness, peace of mind, freedom from pain and fear, in a word your freedom. For what would you sell these things?"[145]

WHOEVER LOOKS OUTSIDE, DREAMS; WHOEVER LOOKS INSIDE, AWAKENS

What lies behind us and before us are tiny matters compared to what lies within us. Your vision will become clear when you look into your heart.

ONLY IN SILENCE CAN WE LISTEN TO THE HEART

As a Japanese proverb says, "Unspoken words are the flowers of silence."[146] In Indonesia and Singapore, some of our friends used to say that you learn more in an hour of silence than you will in a year from books. Others believe silence is more powerful than proving your point. So, beware of demagogues, do your objective analyses to the best of your ability, and for important issues, remember that truth is generally simple and silent.

THE CONQUEROR OF ONESELF IS THE GREATEST OF CONQUERORS

As it is said in Latin, "Vincit qui se vincit" ("he conquers who conquers himself"). Also remember that between acquiring more possessions or more consciousness, choose the latter.

The way to find balance in your own life could be a compilation of these strategies. You might carve out new ones that work for you, too. If you're not sure where to start, try experimenting with one or

---

145 David Cook, "Daily Stoic Life—Protect Your Peace of Mind," February 12, 2020, https://www.lucidwisdom.me/daily-stoic-life-protect-your-peace-of-mind/.

146 Abe Namiko, "Flowers in Japanese Proverbs," Thoughtco, February 5, 2019, https://www.thoughtco.com/japanese-flowers-in-proverbs-2028030.

two of these examples. Over time, you'll find the practices that work best for you. And remember it's a journey, so you can always start small, add some more habits, and seek to have the right amount of work, rest, and leisure every day or week.

PART 2

UPGRADE YOUR MONEY

© Glasbergen/ glasbergen.com

**Investments and
Financial Services**

"When I lose weight, I always gain it right back.
It's the same for losing money, right?"

CHAPTER 12

THE BASICS OF SMARTER INVESTING

In the previous chapters, I've shared insights, quotes, and personal experiences related to personal and professional growth. In this chapter and those that follow, I'd like to spend some time looking more specifically at ways to upgrade your money. With a double degree in business administration and economics, an MBA from IESE, a master's in finance from CEF, and having participated in several programs at Harvard Business School, Stanford, MIT, and Berkeley, among others, along with living in over ten countries in Asia, Europe, and the Americas, managing teams with more than twenty nationalities, and spending more than twenty years in strategy consulting, international business development, digital entrepreneurship, and alternative investing, I have seen firsthand how companies and values can change. With the right analysis and added value, private equity and assets can appreciate over time. If you're able to be a part of that growth, or own it in some way, you'll be able to benefit financially.

SMARTER ALTERNATIVE INVESTMENTS

Of course, it's not just about increasing your money. Certainly, there is freedom that can come from having a certain level of wealth, but there is also a special fulfillment when you positively impact the stakeholders of companies and industries.

For me, I have found great satisfaction in assisting others who want to upgrade their purpose, their companies, and their money. As an investor myself, I have learned to identify real leaders, watch trends carefully, and to listen to customers. I follow what experts say on a daily basis and pay attention to new technologies—after all, advancements serve an important purpose. They help us to think creatively outside the box, to explore new possibilities, and to find incredible opportunities to impact many others. In some cases, this can be done in a transgenerational way.

That's why, when I speak of investing, I like to point out that it really is an active commitment. You might hear of "passive income," which is the idea that investments can generate earnings and interest on their own. The income from them comes to you while you do other activities. It arrives "passively," and some experts will claim you can "make money while you sleep."

Instead of this quiet, complacent approach, I have found that investing needs a high level of involvement. There is research that has to be done on companies, management, and assets. There is due diligence to carry out, and work needed to find out more information from experts. You can add value by contributing your experience, tapping your network, finding financing, and constantly monitoring how the investments are performing. Of course, these days there is technology that can help us do some of these tasks, and I'll speak of that in later chapters. For now, my point is that smarter investments need to be active.

For this reason, you can expect your own investments to be a learning process. You might read a lot of books and talk to many others who have more knowledge than you before beginning. If you don't have the time or feel you are not able to do this entire laborious process of capturing and processing information on your own, I encourage you to work with someone who has experience.

More importantly, the world is changing faster than ever, and sticking to traditional ways of investing could cause you to miss out on some amazing opportunities to achieve higher impacts and returns. It's a bit like walking into an Apple store and asking for a phone that is not a smartphone. You could get a device that works, but you won't have access to some of the latest features that can really uplevel your experience. In terms of investing, this means being open to both historical methods such as value investing, fundamental analysis and asymmetric or uncorrelated investments, as well as up-and-coming trends, which are based on recent technology advancements, such as tokenization, DeFis, AI, machine learning (ML), and quantum computing.

Smarter investments include alternative investments, on average the most profitable ones. I'll explain these further in the following chapters. For now, remember that alternative investments refer to those that are not stocks, bonds, or cash.

Diversification is a key to success in the investing world, so you may opt for a mix of stocks and alternative investments. It is a complex, changing area, and that means you'll be continually learning.

As a good starting point, we'll spend some time looking at investment basics. I'll list out some recommended reading and quotes on approaches to take for investing. I'll also share insights on securities, to give you a taste of how these work and how you might get involved. Then, as I mentioned, the following chapter will help us look at some of the different aspects of investing and understand the changes that are taking place, which are transforming the financial industry.

While you read through the following sections, think about what you might want to do to find your own way in the investing world. It's a path that can upgrade your money and certainly provide a higher return than a savings account at a bank (or stuffed under your mattress). You'll have decisions to make, and the path you take could impact your household in a big way. It could even be a way to leave a legacy for the generations to come and make a difference in society as well as in the lives of your children, grandchildren, and loved ones.

INVESTMENT

Think of investing as a long journey. Before you make a move, read at least one of the most famous books on investment. Reading about investing is one of the highest-return activities you can do. Not only can you learn about how to approach investing smartly from some of the world's best all-time investors, but you can also avoid some of the pitfalls that can sink you early on in your journey. In fact, smart investing is about minimizing risk, limiting your downside, and enjoying unlimited upside. As Warren Buffett famously stated, "Rule #1 is never lose money. Rule #2 is never forget Rule #1."[147]

It may also be helpful to learn what others consider to be best practices for investing. The following list of suggestions comes from the book *The Holy Grail of Investing* by Tony Robbins, a world-renowned entrepreneur, investor, and philanthropist:[148]

---

147 Alisa Wolfson, "This Is Warren Buffett's 'First Rule' about Investing," MarketWatch, January 4, 2024, https://www.marketwatch.com/picks/this-is-warren-buffetts-first-rule-about-investing-heres-what-to-do-if-your-financial-adviser-breaks-that-rule.

148 Tony Robbins, *The Holy Grail of Investing* (New York: Simon & Schuster, 2024).

- Look for opportunities with "asymmetric" risk rewards. Simply put, these investors look for investments where the potential reward far exceeds the downside risk.

- Top investors play the game with an edge. The edge of some special asset access!

- According to Ray Dalio, the Holy Grail is a portfolio of eight to twelve uncorrelated (or non-correlated) investments, which, together, will dramatically reduce risk without sacrificing returns. Dalio demonstrates that a portfolio structured this way can reduce risk by as much as 80 percent while maintaining the same, or similar, upside potential.

- This explains the massive shift to private investments. They simply offer a greater opportunity set. You have to fish where the fish are. In fact, back in 2009, 81 percent of public companies were profitable (post IPO); by 2021, only 28 percent were profitable (post IPO).

- Since 1960, we have had nine recessions, and residential real estate prices only dropped during one of those, the Great Recession of 2008.

- In private equity, we create alpha after buying a company by rolling up our sleeves and adding value.

- Culture is everything. For example, at Goldman Sachs they have this thing called the "TIE" ethos: Teamwork, Integrity, and Excellence. Those are the three themes that bind the firm together.

- It's not about being the smartest person in the room. It's about being a good partner to the person on the other side of the table.

- It's human nature to think if you haven't sold it, you haven't realized your investments. You sell your gains, and you hold on to your losses hoping they get better. That is a terrible strategy in the stock market, as well as in real estate.

When it comes to securities, which could be part of a diversified portfolio, you'll have decisions to make. It's worth putting in the time to thoroughly research companies—or finding someone who can invest on your behalf. You can also learn from the best, and continually follow top investors to see what they are doing and why.

Warren Buffett, in an interview, explained the three basic methods of capital deployment. They are:

1. Start-ups: Even if they don't make a lot of money, start-ups often invest a lot of money in their businesses. At this point, they often need to raise money, but if they can convince investors of their profit potential, they'll be able to secure funding to make it happen. It's not a good indicator of whether a company will continue in this way well into its existence.

2. Companies that are profitable: These companies invest cash to increase their returns. This is how many companies operate.

3. Companies that will eventually generate exponential returns: This type of business doesn't need more funding, and investors receive years of returns on their initial investment. Look for this type of business to invest in.[149]

In the following quotes, you'll learn about the basics of securities and how to approach investing in companies. Use these as you build your own strategy for investing. And remember, there is so much

---

149 Jennifer Saibil, "Warren Buffett's Favorite Companies Have 1 Thing in Common," Fool.com, March 5, 2024, https://www.fool.com/investing/2024/03/05/ warren-buffetts-favorite-companies-have-1-thing-in/.

more to learn. At the end of this book, I've included a list of suggested investment books. Before you start investing, please read at least one of those.

SECURITIES

DON'T BE AFRAID TO INVEST; BE AFRAID IF YOU DON'T

Not investing means not building wealth. The S&P 500 has returned an annualized average return of around 9 percent over the past twenty-five years (and private equity has outperformed it by over five percentage points, i.e., 14 percent).[150] And it's never been easier to start investing. The best stock trading apps no longer charge commissions on stock and ETF (exchange traded funds) trades. Investing platforms offer intuitive research tools and educational resources. Even a dollar can compound over time—but you need to invest it!

START INVESTING THE SOONER THE BETTER
AND GRADUALLY INCREASE THE AMOUNT

Consider an index fund with rock-bottom costs or a specific fund that holds a portfolio that represents your preferred market sector. And if as a business owner you need to learn to be patient, as an investor, you need to learn to control your emotions. Put your money to work as soon as possible since it will work 24/7 and harder than you (and will not fall ill or take a vacation).

---

150 Vartika Gupta, David Kohn, Tim Koller, and Werner Rehm, "Prime Numbers: Markets Will Be Markets: An Analysis of Long-Term Returns from the S&P 500," McKinsey & Company, https://www.mckinsey.com/capabilities/strategy-and-corporate-finance/our-insights/the-strategy-and-corporate-finance-blog/markets-will-be-markets-an-analysis-of-long-term-returns-from-the-s-and-p-500.

CONSIDER DOLLAR-COST AVERAGING

Dollar-cost averaging involves investing the same amount of money in a target security at regular intervals over a certain period of time, regardless of price. By using dollar-cost averaging, investors may lower their average cost per share and reduce the impact of volatility on their portfolios.

DON'T LET THE CEOS FOOL YOU; LET THE BUSINESS'S NUMBERS DO THE TALKING

Pay attention to potential new regulations and interest rate trends and keep a middle- to long-term approach. As Benjamin Graham said, "In the short run, the market is a voting machine, but in the long run, it is a weighing machine."[151] And remember Marty Whitman's investment philosophy, "We don't pay attention to quarterly earnings or consensus forecasts. That's performance investing, not value investing."[152]

FORGET ABOUT PREDICTING THE MARKET; FIND UNDERVALUED COMPANIES AND HAVE PATIENCE

As Howard Marks put it, "Smart investing doesn't consist of buying good assets, but of buying assets well."[153] There is also Charlie Munger's insight, which states, "A lot of people think that if they have a hundred stocks they're investing more professionally than they are if they have four or five. I regard this as insanity."[154]

---

151 Benjamin Graham, "Benjamin Graham Quotes," Goodreads.com, https://www.goodreads.com/quotes/831517-in-the-short-run-the-market-is-a-voting-machine.

152 Mary Whitman, "Mary Whitman Quotes," Novel Investor, https://novelinvestor.com/quote-author/marty-whitman/.

153 Howard Marks, "Howard Marks Quotes," Novel Investor, https://novelinvestor.com/quote-author/howard-marks/.

154 "Munger Games: Charlie Munger's Legacy," RIA Valuation Insights, https://mercer-capital.com/riavaluationinsights/munger-games-charlie-mungers-legacy/.

SMART INVESTORS BUY FROM PESSIMISTS
AND SELL TO OPTIMISTS

Wait for the right price and the right moment. In Joel Greenblatt's words, "The market's very emotional but over time, doing something logical and systematic does work. The market eventually gets it right."[155]

ALL SMART INVESTING IS VALUE INVESTING

I didn't say this—Charlie Munger did, but I agree. And he also used to point out, "Why should it be easy to do something that, if you do it well, two or three times, will make your family rich for life?"[156]

ONCE YOU LEARN PATIENCE, YOUR
OPTIONS SUDDENLY EXPAND

Or as Warren Buffett describes it, "The stock market is a device for transferring money from the impatient to the patient."[157] His right-hand Charlie Munger stated, "A lot of people with high IQs are terrible investors because they've got terrible temperaments. And that is why we say that having a certain kind of temperament is more important than brains. You need to keep raw irrational emotion under control. You need patience and discipline and an ability to take losses and adversity without going crazy."[158] Also, after reading so many biographies, I think that the people who have reached the highest plateaus

---

155 Joel Greenblatt, "Joel Greenblatt Quotes," Novel Investor, https://novelinvestor.com/quote-author/joel-greenblatt.

156 Charlie Munger, "Charlie Munger Quotes," QuoteFancy.com, https://quotefancy.com/quote/1562117/Charlie-Munger-Why-should-it-be-easy-to-do-something-that-if-done-well-two-or-three-times.

157 "The Buffett Way" Profit through Patience," WealthDesk, https://wealthdesk.in/blog/the-buffett-way-profit-through-patience/.

158 Charlie Munger, "Charlie Munger Quotes," Goodreads.com, https://www.goodreads.com/quotes/7237600-a-lot-of-people-with-high-iqs-are-terrible-investors.

as human beings are those who experienced a lot of adversity, dealt with it, and moved on.

WATCH YOUR BUDGET

As Thomas Jefferson said, "Never spend money before you have it."[159]

THREE MAIN RULES FOR INVESTING: #1 DIVERSIFICATION, #2 STOP LOSS, #3 DEFINED PERIOD OF TIME BEFORE INVESTING

Select those multi-baggers (an equity stock that provides more than a 100 percent return) or compounding companies with strong fundamentals that generate exponential returns and that are most likely to continue leading in their industries for the following ten years. Cut your losses at 8 percent below your purchase price, and sell your worst-performing stocks, among the profitable ones, when they are up 25 percent.

MOST MILLIONAIRES GOT THERE BY INVESTING IN SECURITIES, REAL ESTATE, AND SELF-FUNDED BUSINESSES

When investing in securities, at the beginning, consider index funds since they have, in general, beaten mutual funds over time.[160] If you prefer active investing, then follow the value investing criteria and Peter Lynch's recommendation: "Don't buy 'cheap' stocks just because they're cheap. Buy them because the fundamentals are improving."[161]

159 Thomas Jefferson, "Thomas Jefferson Quotes," BrainyQuote.com, https://www. brainyquote.com/quotes/thomas_jefferson_165957.

160 Jean Folger, "Investing in Index Funds: What You Need to Know," Investopedia, August 2, 2023, https://www.investopedia.com/investing-in-index-funds.

161 Peter Lynch, "Peter Lynch Quotes," Novel Investor, https://novelinvestor.com/ quote-author/peter-lynch/.

NEVER INVEST MORE THAN YOU CAN AFFORD, AND NEVER GO INTO DEBT TO INVEST (WITH SOME EXCEPTIONS FOR REAL ESTATE OPPORTUNITIES)

By the way, if a friend or family member borrows from you for the first time, and you can lend the asked amount, do it, but if they don't pay you back, it's over. Don't trip over the same stone twice.

INVESTING IS A BORING LONG-TERM GAME

As Warren Buffett suggests, "Only buy something that you'd be perfectly happy to hold if the market shuts down for ten years."[162] Or as George Soros likes to say, "If you're having fun, you're probably not making money. Good investing is boring."[163] So, begin long-term investing part of your money initially with an index fund with low fees and a portfolio that mimics the stock market, and don't fret when the market falls (it will). Finally, once you have at least ten years of experience investing, as Charlie Munger, vice chairman of Berkshire Hathaway used to say, "Success means being very patient, but aggressive when it's time."[164]

LEARN ABOUT OPTIONS, COVERED CALL STRATEGIES, ETFS, AND REITS

Diversify your portfolio around 30 percent in your own businesses/dividend stocks/trading, 30 percent ETFs, 30 percent real estate/REITs (Real Estate Investment Trusts), and the remaining 10 percent

---

162 Keith Speights, "Warren Buffett Turns 93 Today: Here's His Best Investing Advice Ever," Motley Fool, August 30, 2023, https://www.fool.com/investing/2023/08/30/warren-buffett-turns-93-best-investing-advice-ever2.

163 Aditi Mittal, "Habits of a Good Investor," LinkedIn, August 31, 2023, https://www.linkedin.com/pulse/habits-good-investor-aditi-mittal-cfe/.

164 Charlie Munger, "Charlie Munger Quotes," QuoteFancy.com, https://quotefancy.com/quote/1561885/Charlie-Munger-Most-people-are-too-fretful-they-worry-to-much-Success-means-being-very.

for cash ready for new opportunities. And never stop learning, especially about investment alternatives. In general, you need one hundred hours of learning and practice to be good, one thousand to be very good, and over ten thousand hours to become an expert (and fortunately you can always learn something new, whatever the hours invested, so don't worry about being bored).

THE BEST INVESTMENT YOU CAN MAKE IS IN YOURSELF

Don't skimp on continuing education and learn about all kinds of investments. As Charlie Munger liked to say, "Lifelong learning is paramount to long-term success."[165]

Now that we've seen the basics of smarter investing, it's worth our time to explore additional aspects of it. I've covered how smart investing has the potential to make an impact and give you financial freedom. It's also helpful to know about the possible strategies you can apply, and what opportunities we now have thanks to recent advancements. We'll look at all this in the coming chapters.

---

165 Gautam Baid, "Joys of Compounding," Goodreads.com, https://www.goodreads. com/author/quotes/18960770.Gautam_Baid?page=2#:~:text=Charlie%20 Munger%20said%20that%20lifelong,on%20what%20we%20already%20know.

"Diversification is important. The more
investments you have, the longer it takes
to figure out how much you've lost."

CHAPTER 13

THE RELEVANCE OF THE LONG TERM

I've been actively investing for decades, and the only regret I have is that I didn't start even sooner. That's because I've spent significant time educating myself on best practices. I've read multiple books and shareholders' newsletters, followed top investors to understand their strategies, listened to podcasts, and analyzed my own track record. One point that comes clear, in nearly every resource and experience about investing, is the power of the long-term approach.

I'm not alone—in fact, this is backed by research. If you're eager to jump in and play the market, it could seem exciting to try to make a quick return. Be aware, however, that making a profit in this space can be difficult, and often is not possible. The study "Do Day Traders Rationally Learn about Their Ability?" conducted by the universities of Berkeley, California, and Peking, looked at the effects of short-term trading.[166] Researchers involved in the study analyzed a database with hundreds of thousands of accounts belonging to day traders. The results showed that less than 2 percent of short-term speculators made money each year. In other words, 98 percent lost money!

Table 4: Day Trading by Occasional Traders, First Time Traders, Unprofitable Traders, and Profitable Traders

Occasional day traders are those with less than 20 days of day trading or a one year break in day trading. First timers are day traders who started within the calendar year. Unprofitable (profitable) day traders have a minimum of 20 days of day trading experience through year t-1 and a negative (positive) mean daily day trading return net of costs.

Year	Occasional Traders	First Timers	Unprofitable Traders	Profitable Traders	All Traders
	Panel A: Percentage of All Traders				Number
1995	47.6	41.1	10.4	0.9	136,879
1996	46.1	38.0	14.8	1.1	146,109
1997	32.4	58.5	8.6	0.5	354,057
1998	42.3	40.3	16.5	0.9	399,407
1999	43.7	33.4	21.8	1.1	416,815
2000	42.0	35.5	21.3	1.2	519,343
2001	45.5	24.8	27.7	2.0	430,638
2002	44.0	25.7	28.2	2.1	465,378
2003	42.6	19.7	35.3	2.4	386,450
2004	43.1	22.8	32.1	1.9	431,908
2005	40.6	16.1	40.7	2.6	305,777
2006	45.0	18.9	34.1	2.0	357,877
MEAN	42.9	31.2	24.3	1.6	362,553

---

166 Brad Barber, Yi-Tsung Lee, Yu-Jane Liu, Terrance Odean, and Ke Zhang, "Do Day Traders Rationally Learn about Their Ability?" Berkeley, October 2017, https://faculty. haas.berkeley.edu/odean/papers/Day%20Traders/Day%20Trading%20and%20 Learning%2020110217.pdf.

Think about this a bit more and it becomes more apparent just how hard it can be to trade daily and be successful. The study's findings didn't show that 98 percent failed to beat the market or broke even. These individuals, who traded constantly and tried to make a return, actually ended up with less than when they started. They could have had more in their accounts simply by holding on to their funds, and not investing them at all.

You might be asking, "How does long-term investing compare to this?" To answer that question, again by drawing on research, we see that the results are typically better. The average long-term stock market return is 6.7 percent every year, after accounting for inflation.[167]

Still, there are different ways you can approach long-term investing, and it's worth spending time to see the returns that different types of investors get over time. We'll also look at how simple interest works, and compare it to compound interest, to see the different rates that are available (and to help you choose the right one!). Finally, knowing about taxes can help you make much smarter investment decisions, so we'll cover that as well.

EDUCATION AND EXPERIENCE COUNT

While an annual return of 6.7 percent on stocks is average, there are ways to get more (or less) from the market. I've seen that an experienced, educated investor can earn between 10 and 15 percent every

---

167   Wharton Staff, "Seigel vs. Shiler: Is the Stock Market Overvalued?" Wharton, September 18, 2018, https://knowledge.wharton.upenn.edu/article/siegel-shiller-stock-market/.

year. The annual return of Warren Buffett, one of the best investors in history, is 20 percent.[168]

Statistics show that for the average small investor, the return on stocks is lower than the overall average of 6.7 percent (which takes into account the higher returns from experienced investors). If you are a small investor, you can expect an average return of 2.5 percent from the stock market.[169] While this may seem low, at least part of your purchasing power, depending on the inflation, is preserved. And you won't fall into the category of 98 percent of day traders who lose money.

Still, if you're starting out and want to increase your return so it is higher than 2.5 percent every year on average, I encourage you to read and learn. As I've mentioned, data shows that experienced and educated investors can earn between 7.5 and 12.5 percent more than the small average investor. I have included a list of resources at the end of this book that you can use to grow further in your knowledge. I'll also share some insights here to get you started.

First and foremost, what do extraordinary investors with returns of more than 20 percent have in common? They all invest over the long term and apply value investing strategies (we'll look at value investing in chapter 14).

168 Dr. James Fox, "Starting with Nothing in 2024? I'd Use the Warren Buffett Method to Build Wealth," Yahoo!Finance, January 8, 2024, https://uk.finance.yahoo.com/news/starting-nothing-2024-d-warren-060000213.html.

169 Sean Hanlon, "Why the Average Investor's Investment Return Is So Low," Forbes, April 24, 2014, https://www.forbes.com/sites/advisor/2014/04/24/why-the-average-investors-investment-return-is-so-low/.

The World's Top Investors		
Investor, Key Fund/Vehicle	Period	Average Annual Returns After Fees
Jim Simmons, Medallion	1988-2018	39%
George Soros, Quantum	1969-2000	32%
Steven Cohen, SAC	1992-2003	30%
Peter Lynch, Magellan	1977-1990	29%
Warren Buffett, Berkshire Hathaway	1965-2018	21%
Ray Dalio, Pure Alpha	1991-2018	12%

Source: The Wall Street Journal, www.libertythroughwealth.com

These legends have also identified market patterns, and learned the power of compound interest and how it can lead to higher earnings as the years pass.

UNDERSTANDING SIMPLE INTEREST

If you make an investment with a simple interest rate attached to the earnings, you'll want to know what to expect as a return. Simple interest is calculated by taking the initial principal amount, without adding in any interest that may have accrued in the past. To find the return to expect, take the initial sum of money, multiply it by the interest rate and then by the time it is invested.

The formula is:

Simple Interest = $P \times r \times t$

where

P represents the principal amount (the initial sum of money)

r represents the interest rate

t represents the time the money is invested, usually in years

For example, if you invest $10,000 at a simple interest rate of 5 percent for five years, the interest earned would be:

Interest = 10,000 × 0.05 × 5

The total amount of interest your investment would earn after five years would be $2,500. In all, your investment after five years would be $12,500.

Simple interest grows at a linear pace, so the interest you earn over time will be the same every year. Once you know how much you'll earn from it in a year, you can expect that same amount the following year. While this may be easy to calculate, it also limits some of your earning potential, as the rate won't be based on the amount that accumulates over time.

UNDERSTANDING COMPOUND INTEREST

Unlike simple interest, compound interest factors in the interest that accrues over time. The interest rate is applied both to the principal amount and to the interest that has been previously earned. This allows the investment to grow exponentially.

To calculate compound interest, the formula is:

$C_n = C_0 \times (1 + i)n$

C_n = Capital (the amount) you'll have at the end of the year

C_0 = Starting capital (the amount you initially invested)

i = annual interest rate

n = number of years

Following the example from the simple interest section, if you invest $10,000 at a compound interest rate of 5 percent for five years, the interest earned would be:

$C_n = 10,000 \times (1 + 0.05)5$

C = $12,762.82

The total amount of interest your investment would earn over five years would be $2,762.82. In all, your investment would be $12,762.82 after that period.

THE ADVANTAGES OF COMPOUND INTEREST

Viewing the simple interest example compared to the compound interest one, we see that with compound interest your investment would earn $262.82 over five years. Over time, and at higher interest rates, the differences are greater.

Consider the following chart, which shows $10,000 invested at several simple interest rates for fifty years:

RETURN ON 10,000 EUROS IN 50 YEARS WITH SIMPLE INTEREST

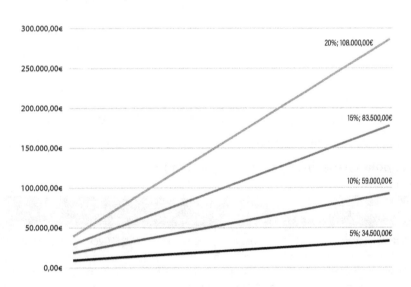

Now look at the next chart, which depicts a $10,000 investment with different compound interest rates for fifty years:

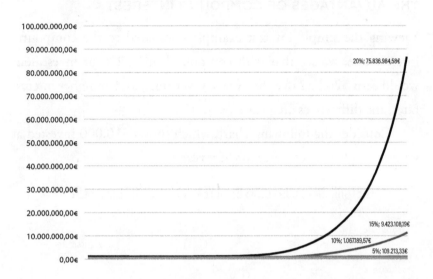

RETURN ON 10,000 EUROS IN 50 YEARS WITH COMPOUND INTEREST

To see how simple interest compares to compound interest over time, consider the following graph. It shows the information from the previous charts displayed next to each other:

10.000€ OVER 50 YEARS	5%	10%	15%	20%
Simple Interest	34.500,00€	59.000,00€	83.500,00€	108.000,00€
Compound Interest	109.213,33€	1.067.189,57€	9.423.108,19€	75.836.984,58€
Difference	316,56%	1808,80%	11285,16%	70219,43%

When investing for the long term, compound interest allows your funds to grow exponentially. As Albert Einstein said, "Compound interest is the eighth wonder of the world. He who understands it, earns it ... he who doesn't ... pays it."[170]

LONG-TERM INVESTING AND TAXES

When we make an investment and don't take out earnings, we can defer paying taxes on the amount. In fact, we won't have to go to a taxman until we sell our shares. When we do sell, if we have held the stocks for longer than a year, they will usually be subject to long-term capital gains tax rates, which could be lower than short-term gains tax rates.

On the other hand, if we speculate in the short term, and buy and sell stocks within a year, the earnings need to be reported as short-term capital gains. In many tax systems, short-term capital gains are taxed much more heavily than long-term capital gains. (And that's if you make something from day trading! Remember that only 2 percent of short-term speculators didn't lose money in the study by Berkeley, California, and Peking.)[171]

As a final thought, and one that could motivate you to start long-term investing today, consider the example of Jim Simons. His trading strategy is described in the book *The Man Who Solved the Market: How Jim Simons Launched the Quant Revolution.*[172] I highly recommend reading this guide to see his strategies. In summary, he didn't look to be right 100 percent of the time. Instead, he tried to

170   Albert Einstein, "Albert Einstein Quotes," Goodreads.com, https://www.goodreads.com/quotes/76863-compound-interest-is-the-eighth-wonder-of-the-world-he.

171   Brad Barber, Yi-Tsung Lee, Yu-Jane Liu, Terrance Odean, and Ke Zhang, "Do Day Traders Rationally Learn about Their Ability?" Berkeley, October 2017, https://faculty.haas.berkeley.edu/odean/papers/Day%20Traders/Day%20Trading%20and%20Learning%2020110217.pdf.

172   Gregory Zuckerman, *The Man Who Solved the Market: How Jim Simons Launched the Quant Revolution* (London: Portfolio, 2019).

have a small edge or to be right 50.75 percent of the time. With this strategy, he found he could make a lot of money. Since 1988, his flagship Medallion Hedge Fund has generated an average annual return of 66 percent. It has done this by finding the hidden patterns in the market and making between 150,000 and 300,000 trades a day. His investment profits far exceed those of Warren Buffett, George Soros, and Peter Lynch. According to estimates, his latest firm, called Renaissance, has earned profits of more than $100 billion.[173]

Once you've thought about smarter investing and taken a long-term approach, it's time to consider which companies to invest in. I'll share guidelines on this in the following chapter, which will cover value investing. This refers to focusing on the potential growth and future worth of a company. In the meantime, reflect on your own finances and develop a starting strategy to upgrade your money on your own terms over the long run. And remember, play iterated games. All the returns in life, whether in wealth, knowledge, or relationships, come from compound interest.

173 Gregory Zuckerman, "The Man Who Solved the Market: The Notes," Novel Investor, https://novelinvestor.com/notes/the-man-who-solved-the-market-by-gregory-zuckerman/.

"Sometimes the best investments are the
ones you don't make. Let's go with that
strategy and see where it takes us."

CHAPTER 14

VALUE INVESTING

When it comes to investing in companies, it's not just about holding stocks for the long term. It's also about picking the right ones. Which companies are going to grow in value over time? How many will likely have the same profits during the next few years? Which ones will use capital so wisely that it eventually generates exponential returns? Which others could be headed on a downward spiral, leading to fewer profits or even failure?

Philip Fisher, a renowned investor, is often considered a pioneer of the growth investment strategy. He was the first to look at the emerging value of a company, rather than its current stock price. He based his decisions on a thorough analysis that aimed to understand the firm and its potential for growth.

Fisher was born in 1907 in San Francisco, California, and graduated from Stanford University with a degree in economics. After working as a securities analyst, he founded his investment firm Fisher & Co. in 1931. Fisher managed the firm for almost seventy years, when he retired in 1999. During his time there, he was known for delivering strong returns on behalf of his clients. He influenced other great investors, including Warren Buffett.[174]

Rather than trying to follow business cycles and buy at low prices to later sell at high ones, Fisher introduced the concept of "buy and hold." He even wrote, "It is only occasionally that there is any reason for selling at all." Following his own teachings, Fisher purchased stock in Motorola in 1955 and held on to the shares until his death in 2004.[175]

To share his philosophy for value investing, Fisher wrote *Common Stocks and Uncommon Profits and Other Writings,* a book I highly recommend reading. In the pages, Fisher reveals his Fifteen Point Strategy, which are fifteen points that investors can use to assess a company. I regularly turn to this checklist when considering an investment (in addition to the positive impact I want to see a firm making in the world).[176] While Fisher says that most companies don't perfectly meet all fifteen points, carrying out this exercise can help you better understand the potential growth and value of a company. Once you find a good fit, you could purchase shares—and then watch them grow over time, without ever selling.

Certainly, this requires rigorous research and much more than a quick Google search. I'm sharing the fifteen points here in this chapter, as they are often referenced and followed by other successful investors. You'll find a short description added to each of the points as well.

As you read through these, think about stocks you may have been thinking about investing in. Also evaluate your current investment strategy. And remember, if you don't have the time to commit

---

174 James Chen, "Philip Fisher: History, Market Impact, FAQs," Investopedia, January 2, 2024, https://www.investopedia.com/terms/p/philip-fisher.asp.

175 "Common Stock Checklist from Phil Fisher," Old School Value, https://www.old-schoolvalue.com/investing-strategy/common-stock-checklist/#google_vignette.

176 Philip Fisher, *Common Stocks and Uncommon Profits and Other Writing* (Hoboken: Wiley, 1996).

to carrying out this legwork, find a trusted investor who can actively invest on your behalf. After all, that's what Fisher did for his clients during the decades he ran his firm.

Here are the fifteen points from Fisher's book *Common Stocks and Uncommon Profits*:

1. DOES THE COMPANY OFFER PRODUCTS OR SERVICES WITH SUFFICIENT COMMERCIAL POTENTIAL TO MAKE A SUBSTANTIAL INCREASE IN SALES POSSIBLE FOR AT LEAST SEVERAL YEARS?

Don't just check how a company performed last year. Look at their track record to see if they have been expanding or shrinking during the last several years. They should have products and services that can serve a much bigger customer base (the famous total addressable market). This way they have an opportunity to produce more revenue and profits in the coming years.

2. IS MANAGEMENT DETERMINED TO CONTINUE TO DEVELOP PRODUCTS OR PROCESSES THAT WILL FURTHER INCREASE SALES POTENTIAL WHEN THE GROWTH POTENTIAL OF CURRENTLY ATTRACTIVE PRODUCT LINES HAVE BEEN LARGELY EXPLOITED?

Markets eventually mature, and products that are attractive today may not be purchased tomorrow. It's important to have a management team in place that is already looking to the future. They will be developing new products that can be sold in the years to come, and possibly replace their current offerings.

3. HOW EFFECTIVE ARE THE COMPANY'S RESEARCH AND DEVELOPMENT EFFORTS RELATIVE TO ITS SIZE?

Check out a company's competitors and find out the size of their research and development departments. Look to see if the company's research efforts have increased or decreased during the last years. All of these can be signs to show you if the company believes they have a strong footing in the market, and don't need to develop as many new innovations, or if they are trying hard to compete and improve their position by creating something different.

4. DOES THE COMPANY HAVE AN ABOVE-AVERAGE SALES ORGANIZATION?

Even if a firm produces a great product, it will need to actively work on branding and selling. Look at how it advertises and connects with its customers. Consider the reviews you can find about its products and its level of customer satisfaction. This will help you understand how their goods and customer service are perceived in the market.

5. DOES THE COMPANY HAVE A PROFIT MARGIN WORTH CONSIDERING?

Research to see how the company's profit margins compare to others in its industry. If it is reinvesting profits, find out why. Perhaps it is striving to grow during the next few years, or maybe it needs the funds to continue functioning.

6. WHAT DOES THE COMPANY DO TO MAINTAIN OR IMPROVE PROFIT MARGINS?

If a firm simply increases the price of its products to have a better profit margin, this may not be a long-term solution. Look to see what the company is doing to manage costs, and how it plans to scale and increase its profit margins in the future.

7. DOES THE COMPANY HAVE OPTIMAL STAFFING AND EXCELLENT WORKING RELATIONSHIPS?

You can look at online reviews to see what employees are saying about the company. If it's rated as a great place to work, it could have a strong culture that is fostering growth. Firms that have many staff members leaving, or low retention rates, could have underlying problems.

8. DO THE COMPANY'S MANAGERS HAVE EXCELLENT RELATIONSHIPS WITH EACH OTHER?

How the leadership team interacts with one another will have an impact on the company's performance. If they get along well and work as a team, this could set the tone for the departments below them. Tense workplaces could be a sign of a struggling company.

9. DOES THE COMPANY HAVE SUFFICIENT MANAGERIAL CAPACITY?

A company that depends heavily on the leader could be in trouble if that person can no longer carry out their role. Firms with the potential to grow should have responsibilities delegated to lower-level managers. That way, decisions can be made more readily, and changes can be implemented more easily.

10. WHAT IS THE QUALITY OF THE COMPANY'S COST ANALYSIS AND ACCOUNTING CONTROLS?

It may be difficult to find out how a company handles cost analysis and accounting controls, but you can check to see if they carefully track their costs and revenues. If they have detailed records, it could be an indicator that they monitor expenses well. They may also follow what causes costs to go up and analyze events that led to higher revenues, too.

11. ARE THERE OTHER ASPECTS OF THE BUSINESS, SOMEWHAT SPECIFIC TO THE GIVEN INDUSTRY, THAT MAY GIVE CLUES TO THE INVESTOR AS TO HOW EXCEPTIONAL THE COMPANY MAY BE RELATIVE TO ITS COMPETITORS?

Reading a company's annual report could be a good starting point. You'll also want to discover what other information is available about the company, its competitors, and its industry. Look at trade journals, watch videos, and read blogs to learn more about how the company compares to others in its segment.

12. DOES THE COMPANY HAVE A SHORT- OR LONG-TERM FORECAST FOR EARNINGS?

Firms that are looking to the long term will have a different approach than firms that are only thinking short term. A company might give up short-term profits if it is aiming for exponential long-term growth. Amazon, for instance, didn't make a profit for the first nine years of its existence.

13. IN THE FORESEEABLE FUTURE, WILL THE COMPANY'S GROWTH REQUIRE SUFFICIENT EQUITY FUNDING SO THAT THE INCREASED NUMBER OF SHARES THEN OUTSTANDING WILL CANCEL OUT THE PROFIT OF CURRENT SHAREHOLDERS FOR THIS ANTICIPATED GROWTH?

Find out how the company has raised equity in the past. Check if they have increased the number of shares before. If they have, evaluate what the results were, and how shareholders were impacted.

14. DOES MANAGEMENT SPEAK FREELY ABOUT ITS AFFAIRS WHEN THINGS ARE GOING WELL, BUT CLAM UP WHEN PROBLEMS AND DISAPPOINTMENTS ARISE?

You'll want to know if the company leaders have a history of reporting honestly to shareholders. It may be easy to share good news. What happens, though, when things don't go as smoothly? Look for transparency, starting with leadership.

15. DOES THE COMPANY HAVE A MANAGEMENT TEAM WITH UNQUESTIONABLE INTEGRITY?

Managers should be trustworthy and feel a sense of duty toward the shareholders. If a manager lacks integrity, it can be hard to decipher who is really benefiting. Unreliable management teams might look for ways to take profits rather than pass them on to shareholders.

To find the answers to these questions, you'll often have to talk to other people, lean into your network and personal circle, and research on your own. It can take a while to thoroughly analyze a company. It's an important step, though, as it will help you see where the company is today, and how it is set up to face tomorrow.

It may seem impossible to find a company with positive answers to all fifteen points. According to Fisher, a company doesn't have to score perfectly, as that would be very difficult. If a firm meets most of the points, it could be an indicator of a good investment.

By now, you've seen how to invest in a smart way, over the long term, and choosing wisely. It may seem like a lot of work, and it is. As I've mentioned before, if you don't have the time to carry out such an in-depth review of a company before making an investment, find someone who has knowledge, experience, and a great track record. They can help you make decisions and carry out value investing so you can, like Fisher, buy and hold, and then watch the value of your stocks grow.

© Glasbergen/ glasbergen.com

GLASBERGEN

"Why is it so difficult to think outside of the box?
We have no trouble *spending* outside of the box!"

CHAPTER 15

COGNITIVE BIASES, FUTURES, AND OPTIONS

Once you start educating yourself on trading, you might be surprised at how much information is out there! I personally make reading a daily habit and am learning nonstop. I have spent years in the investing world already and have found principles that I follow and that make a difference. Some of these guidelines include being aware of cognitive biases and knowing about futures and options to hedge your investments.

If you're knowledgeable in these areas, you can mitigate your risk in several ways. When you avoid biases, you'll be more likely to make a rational decision, rather than one based on emotion or miscalculation. Knowing about future and advanced option strategies can also help you make the most of relative price movements. You won't have to depend on straight-up price changes, and hope they go in your favor. Instead, you can protect yourself by buying and selling related futures or options.

In the following sections, I'll lay out what you'll want to know about cognitive biases. I'll then explain the basics of futures and options when it comes to investing, to help you understand how they work. While you read through these, you can think about how you tend to make decisions, along with what you plan to do going forward when making an investment.

AVOIDING COGNITIVE BIASES

When we speak of "cognitive biases" in investing, we're referring to alterations in our minds that are hard to eliminate. They can lead to a distorted perception of reality, poor judgment calls, or interpretations that are not logical. Biases can prevent us from making rational decisions when investing.

For this reason, the more you can get rid of biases when making a call about a trade or security, the better. I'll share two lists here, one by Adrián Godás and one by Paco Lodeiro, who together host a recommended podcast called *Value Investing*. Both share advice regularly on how to build wealth through safe and sensible strategies.

According to Adrián Godás,[177] the top ten cognitive biases are:

1. *Comparison by contrast:* Rather than studying a company, we might simply compare it to others to decide how it is performing.
2. *Echo chamber:* This involves being around people who think the same as you on almost every topic.

---

3. *Consistency:* Once we've committed to a stock or made an opinion, we don't want to change our minds or back down, even if the situation changes.

4. *Anchorage:* We can hold on to a specific number, such as the purchase price of a stock. We might base our decision around this value, and not adjust our strategy when new information comes in.

5. *Narratives:* We might make up a story about how an investment will perform, relying on what we think in our minds and not the data that becomes available.

6. *Authority:* We might listen to those we think are in a position of credibility, and not make our decisions based on our own findings.

7. *False consensus bias:* We might overestimate the extent that others agree with us. For instance, we may think that because the people around us own a stock, everyone has it.

8. *Sympathy:* We trust people we like, such as a charismatic leader. The CEO of a company might not be making smart decisions, even if we find them to be a pleasant person.

9. *Availability:* We might place a greater importance on the most recent information about a company, rather than looking at its performance over time.

10. *Status quo:* It can be easy to think that everything will remain the same, and that stock prices won't change.

Now we'll continue with the top ten cognitive biases in investing, according to Paco Lodeiro:[178]

1. *Argumentum ad antiquitatem:* This refers to a thesis that is viewed as correct based on the fact that it has been tradition-

---

178 Ibid.

ally considered to be true. For instance, we might say, "The price of housing always rises," and not research home price trends to see what might happen in the coming year.

2. *Fallacy by association:* This often occurs when we form an opinion based on our perception of a group, rather than a single company. We may decide, "Costco is a great business because it is a retailer," and not evaluate Costco as a single company to see its performance.

3. *Inappropriate generalization or proof by example:* We might use one particular case to form an opinion about an entire industry. For instance, we may decide investing in online companies is risky because of what happened to MySpace, a company that failed.

4. *Argumentum ad verecundiam:* This refers to basing the relevancy of a statement on factors such as the level of fame, prestige, or knowledge of the person making it.

5. *Sunk cost fallacy:* This occurs when someone makes an investment that seems unprofitable and decides they have to keep it, because otherwise they will lose what they have spent so far.

6. *Argumentum verbosium:* This can occur when an argument is so complex, long, or poorly presented that others assume it must be true—and they simply don't understand it.

7. *Biased sample:* A sample from a population might be thought to represent the entire group, even if it truly doesn't.

8. *Simple cause:* We might jump to the conclusion that one event triggered another, when in fact there could be multiple causes that led up to the outcome.

9. *Post hoc:* This biased position assumes that if one event follows another, the second event was caused by the first.

10. *False dilemma:* We could have a situation in which two points of view are considered to be the only options available, when in reality there are others to think about.

In reviewing these biases, you may be able to understand how they can cloud our judgment when making investment decisions. We can easily overestimate the value of a stock or ignore relevant information that could impact our decision. Simply knowing about biases can help us avoid them. Remember to research thoroughly, ask questions (if to expert investors not about their recommendation, but about what they have—or don't have—in their portfolio), and keep a curious mind to make smart choices.

FUTURES SPREAD TRADING AND ADVANCED OPTION STRATEGIES

When investing, you don't have to put everything in one place and hope for the best! In fact, there are various strategies you can use to manage and even mitigate your risk. Some of these involve what is known as futures spread trading and advanced option strategies.

Futures spread trading consists of taking positions in two futures contracts simultaneously, with the goal of making a profit from the difference in price movements between the two contracts. The contracts might be for the same commodity, but have distinct delivery months, which is known as a calendar spread. Or they could be different but related commodities, and this technique is called inter-commodity spread.

When we speak of advanced option strategies, we're referring to financial derivatives that give you the right to buy or sell an asset at a set price (often called a strike price) within a certain time frame. These involve combinations of options contracts, often to hedge against various market conditions. You can give yourself a layer of protection and increase your chances of earning—rather than losing—by having some control over the price and time period.

I'm listing a few examples here of futures spread trading and advanced option strategies to give you an idea of what you might be able to do. Keep in mind these are only a brief overview of the strategies. You'll want to carry out more research before putting them into practice. If you don't have the time or expertise to do so, find someone who has experience and can help you make these kinds of decisions.

- *Bull Call Spread:* This strategy looks for a moderate increase in the price of the underlying asset.
- *Bear Put Spread:* Investors look to benefit from a moderate decrease in the price of the underlying asset.
- *Long Straddle:* Traders use this when they anticipate significant fluctuations in the price of an underlying asset and are not sure how it will move.
- *Short Straddle:* Investors choose this strategy when they expect the price of the underlying asset to remain somewhat stable during the set time frame for their options.
- *Short Strangle:* Traders will sell a call option (the right to buy at a specified price) and a put option (the right to sell at a specified price) at the same set price.
- *Long Calendar Spreads:* Also known as a time spread or horizontal spread, this strategy involves buying and selling options of the same underlying asset with the same set price but different expiration dates.
- *Short Iron Condor:* This consists of two puts (one long and one short), two calls (one long and one short), and four strike prices. They all have the same expiration date.

- *Call Backspread:* Investors will buy a higher number of call options than the number of call options being sold, often because they are feeling bullish but want to limit their risk.

- *Put Backspread:* This strategy involves buying a higher number of put options than the number of put options that are being sold. In this case, investors are bearish but again want to limit their risk.

- *Trading Protective Puts:* Investors use this technique to protect their existing stock holdings by purchasing put options on the same underlying stock that they own.

- *Trading Covered Calls to Generate Income:* Investors will sell call options on the stock they own, and at the same time hold an equivalent number of shares of that stock.

By looking at cognitive biases, futures spread trading, and advanced option strategies, we can see how intricate investing is. While it may sound easy to purchase stock in a company, the reality is that there are many tactics you can employ to both make a profit and reduce your downside risk. As you look into these strategies that I've listed, I hope you find ones that you might be able to put to use. Watch what other investors who you admire are doing and pay attention to how they act. They could provide more clues for you to learn and grow in your own investment journey.

© Glasbergen/ glasbergen.com

**INVESTMENTS AND
RETIREMENT PLANNING**

"Sure, it's possible to make good money from the lottery.
Invest in the company that prints the cards."

CHAPTER 16

THE POTENTIAL OF ALTERNATIVE INVESTMENTS

There is a common saying that goes, "Whatever millionaires do, we all should do it." If that is the case, we should be paying attention to alternative investments. These are investments, which are different from stocks, bonds, and cash (by the way, the worst place to keep your savings is in a bank account). Alternative investments could include hedge funds, private equity, venture capital, and private debt, along with real assets such as real estate, infrastructure, art, and natural resources.

One advantage that alternative investments bring, as we'll see in this chapter, is that they are not strongly related to the performance of stocks, bonds, and cash (also remember the money you have not invested loses its purchasing power due to inflation). This provides a layer of protection, meaning if you have investments in stock and alternatives, one category might perform poorly and the other could do well, thereby offsetting your losses. In addition, alternative investments can provide other advantages. I've found in my own research and practice that alternative investments offer a higher-than-average return over other types of investments. To see how this works, we'll explore what alternative investments are, along with some of the benefits they bring and how you can get started investing in them.

UNDERSTANDING ALTERNATIVE INVESTMENTS

To get an idea of the opportunities available, we'll run through some of the common types of alternative investments. Due to related trends of tokenization and DeFi, which we'll look at more in-depth in the coming chapters, investing in other ways outside of the stock and bond markets is becoming more commonplace. These advancements are also creating more opportunities and greater access for investors. As you read through these descriptions, think about how you might want to get started in this space.

HEDGE FUNDS

Hedge funds usually pool the resources of accredited investors and use the funds to make investments. An accredited investor, at least at the time of writing this book, is someone with a net worth of at least $1 million, excluding their primary residence. It could also be a person who has earned $200,000 (or $300,000 for couples) during the last two years with a reasonable expectation to make the same in the current year.

Hedge funds often tie up investors' money for long periods of time, to be able to establish an investing strategy and carry it out. The return on hedge funds varies greatly, as they can lead to small gains, large gains, small losses, or large losses. They do not need to disclose their activities to the public and are operated as private partnerships. Hedge funds might invest in public markets, for and against companies, and in relative performance.[179]

This investment option is best known for its use of the following techniques:

- *Long-short strategy:* This consists of buying one security and selling another similar security, generating returns not based on the overall performance of the market but on the relative performance of those two securities.
- *Derivatives:* These are contracts to buy or sell a security at a specified price.[180]

PRIVATE EQUITY

Private equity involves providing capital to businesses outside of the public markets. An investor might make a direct investment in a company, or they could make an indirect investment through a private equity fund. Traditionally, private equity has only been accessible to institutions and high-net-worth individuals, based on the high amount that needs to be invested and a holding period.

Private equity firms are known as general partners (GPs), and they collect investment capital from limited partners (LPs) during a funding phase. They then distribute cash back to the LPs during a harvesting period. The time frame often will last for five years, with a total ten-year life of the fund. Private equity is illiquid, as it is not easy to sell or exchange your investment for cash until the fund closes.[181]

The three levers used to increase equity value are:

---

179 Harvard Business School Online: Alternative Investments, file:///C:/Users/marmh/Downloads/HBS%20Online%20Alt%20Investments%20M3%20Takeaway.pdf.

180 Ibid.

181 Harvard Business School Online: Alternative Investments, file:///C:/Users/marmh/Downloads/HBS%20Online%20Alt%20Investments%20M1%20Takeaway.pdf.

- Multiple expansion
- EBITDA growth
- Cash generation (net debt reduction)[182]

The return on private equity could be higher than public markets, but there are risks at play too, and investors will need to thoroughly research the business to determine its current and future value.

VENTURE CAPITAL

Venture capital provides funding for start-ups and other companies that are unable to get bank loans or access the public markets. This is a very illiquid and high-risk type of investment, as the amount provided will be put toward growth for the company. Many businesses fail, so an investor could lose in a substantial way if the plan doesn't work out. Venture capital is usually provided by well-off investors who can afford the risk and waiting involved.

PRIVATE DEBT

Private debt usually refers to loans that are made available to firms with earnings below $100 million. For institutional investors, this option is often attractive, as it can bring higher returns than the public markets. However, it can take time to source deals and the due diligence required is often a long and complex process.

REAL ESTATE

You might see this classified as residential, which usually refers to purchasing a single-family home, or as commercial, which could cover a multifamily building like an apartment or an office, retail, or

---

182 Ibid.

industrial property. Investing in real estate can be carried out in many ways, including a core, added value, or opportunistic style. A core investment usually has lower risk and generates a return based on the income from tenants. An added value has higher risk but aims to make changes to the property to increase its price. Opportunistic has the highest risk, but also could have higher returns if market conditions align. It often involves purchasing land and developing it, overseeing the process from ground-up construction to the completion, and then the rental or sale of it.

INFRASTRUCTURE

Investors might choose to put their funds into the development of resources for a community, such as a hospital, university, transport line, telecom project, or utilities like a water treatment facility. These investments are often low-risk and provide a steady cash flow. However, investors usually need to have substantial funds to be able to participate.

ART

Investors often consider art as a store of value, meaning it can be kept and exchanged in the future without diminishing greatly in value. These investments tend to be long term and can appreciate over time. Another benefit for investors is that they can enjoy the piece of art if they choose to display it in their home or other location where it can be easily viewed. An example of this in action can be seen at FidelitasArte.com.

NATURAL RESOURCES

This asset class covers anything that is mined or collected in raw form. It could be renewable or nonrenewable and is often divided into five categories: energy (including oil and gas), agricultural and farmland, metals and mining, forests, and water. Natural resources are often seen as a store of value, and the demand for them typically increases as an economy expands and incomes rise.

A GROWING TREND

While wealthy individuals do tend to invest part of their portfolios in stocks and bonds, there is much more to their story. As we can see in the following chart, high-net-worth individuals, who are those with more than $1 million in assets, are paying attention to alternative investments. Individuals who are considered to be very high or ultra-high net worth (those with more than $5 million and $30 million, respectively) invest even more in alternatives.

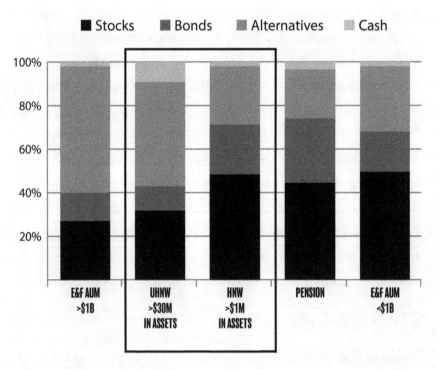

Overall, there is a growing interest in alternative investments. Between 2003 and 2018, the size of the global investment market doubled, and during the same time, alternative investments nearly tripled, according to the Chartered Alternative Investment Analyst (CAIA) Association. Of all the worldwide investments made during that time, 12 percent were allocated to alternative investments.[183]

According to a recent Ernst & Young report from 2024, alternative investments are being adopted by mass affluent investors due to their superior and recurring returns, with 32 percent currently and 48 percent expected by the end of 2024. Even more striking are the percentages of very high net worth individuals (VHNWI)—those with a net worth of at least $5 million—and ultra-high net worth individuals (UHNWI)—those with investable assets of at least $30 million. With 55 percent and 81 percent of current and 68 percent and 85 percent of expected alternative investments respectively, don't you think it's significant that those with the most money have such percentages?

---

183 "Tokenisation of Alternative Investments," CAIA.org, 2021, chrome-extension://
efaidnbmnnnibpcajpcglclefindmkaj/https://caia.org/sites/default/files/2021-02/
CAIA_Tokenisation_of_Alternatives.pdf.

CURRENT USE OF ALTERNATIVE INVESTMENTS VS FUTURE POTENTIAL USE (INCLUDING CONSIDERATION)

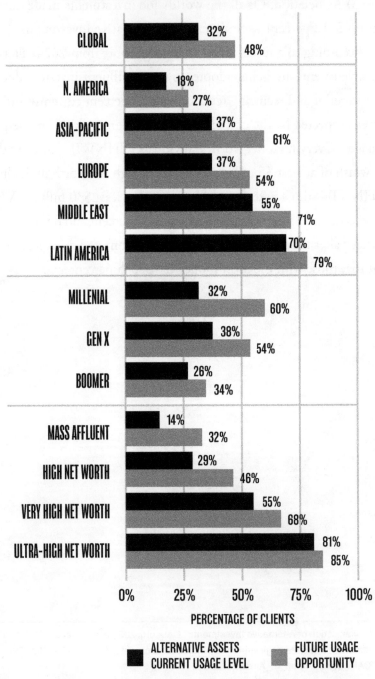

As we can see in the following chart from YieldStreet.com, private markets have a track record of getting much higher returns than stocks during the last fifteen years.

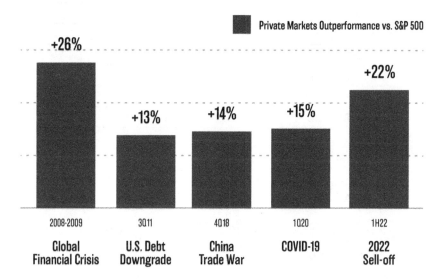

In fact, the average HNW portfolio today has about 25 percent allocated to alternative investments, and these same investments provide almost 50 percent of the returns.

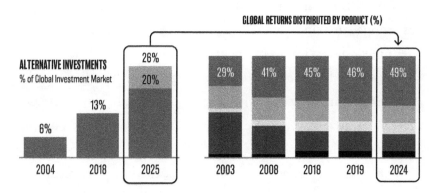

Now you can imagine how some of the world's top investors have averaged annual returns after fees of more than 30 percent for more than thirty years.

The World's Top Investors		
Investor, Key Fund/Vehicle	Period	Average Annual Returns After Fees
Jim Simmons, Medallion	1988-2018	39%
George Soros, Quantum	1969-2000	32%
Steven Cohen, SAC	1992-2003	30%
Peter Lynch, Magellan	1977-1990	29%
Warren Buffett, Berkshire Hathaway	1965-2018	21%
Ray Dalio, Pure Alpha	1991-2018	12%

Source: The Wall Street Journal, www.libertythroughwealth.com

THE APPEAL OF DISTRESSED DEBT

There is one area of real estate investing that has grown in recent years, and we'll touch on it here. Known as distressed debt, the idea is to take advantage of properties that may need repairs or have loans with missed payments. Distressed debt investing includes pre-foreclosure short sales or auctions due to mortgage defaults, non-performing loans (NPLs), and real estate-owned (REO) investments.

An NPL is a mortgage loan in default, meaning the borrower has stopped making payments. A note becomes non-performing after ninety days with no payments. At this point, the lender might choose to sell the note to an investor to get some liquidity and also avoid foreclosure proceedings, which can be costly. Investors may buy these notes because they are usually sold at a discount. So, a note of $200,000 might be sold for $20,000. If an investor can recover the $20,000 and receive more from the loans, the losses are recovered, and any additional amount brought in will be earnings. In addition, since the investor becomes the lender when the note is purchased, the investor could end up foreclosing the property. Any proceedings from a foreclosure sale could add to the earnings as well. If $20,000 is paid and then a foreclosure sale takes place for $150,000, the investor can keep the difference (though there will be costs for the foreclosure proceedings to account for as well).[184]

REOs refer to properties owned by a lender. If an owner of a property with a mortgage defaults, the bank will typically take back the property and try to sell it. This often occurs through a foreclosure auction. If, however, the lender is unable to sell the property for an amount that will help cover the loan, it will take ownership of it instead. The lender will then try to sell the REO through a real estate agent or by listing the property online. REOs are usually sold at a steep discount but they could need ample repairs.[185]

During times of higher interest rates and inflation, it can be tough for borrowers to make their debt payments. Homeowners especially may struggle to make their mortgage payments every month. This can lead to an increase in defaults and foreclosures, creating a ripple effect through the economy. There could be less stability, rising prices, and tighter restrictions on getting financing.

Due to factors like COVID-19, national debt, and higher periods of inflation, there has been an increase in the number of foreclosures in the United States. In January 2023, the delinquency rate for FHA loans, which are loans insured by the Federal Housing Administration, was nearly 5 percent, and grew during the remainder of the year. By the end of 2023, more than one in twenty FHA loans were

---

184   David Garner, "Non Performing Notes: The Ultimate Guide," Garnaco, September 3, 2021, https://garnaco.net/blog/2021/09/03/non-performing-notes/.

185   James Chen, "Real Estate Owned (REO) Definition, Advantages, and Disadvantages," Investopedia, December 16, 2020, https://www.investopedia.com/terms/r/realestateowned.asp.

distressed, and payments were either delinquent by ninety days or more, or the properties were in foreclosure.[186]

When this happens, there are also opportunities for investors to come in and make purchases. Their investments can help revive the economy, as they put capital into the market and help values increase. For me, this coincides with my passion to make a good impact and provide opportunities for others. In addition, investing in distressed debt can help diversify a portfolio. Real estate investments, like related private debt and lending, have a low correlation with stocks and bonds. Property prices are driven by many local factors, such as supply and demand, and the community's economy and job market. So, if you have purchased stocks, buying real estate could help reduce risk, as the performance of the real estate may not coincide with the performance of the stocks.

SETTING AN ALTERNATIVE STRATEGY

When an investor comes up to me and asks how many companies and stocks I suggest investing in, I respond, "a maximum of three businesses and three to nine stocks." It's important to have an investing philosophy. Mine, as I mentioned, is to have few investments, to be able to add value and follow them, selecting those that can make a positive social impact, ideally a transgenerational one.

Learning about psychology is critical, whatever your business or investment philosophy, since we make decisions emotionally and then justify them rationally. Sometimes subjective reality can transform objective reality. For example, when a sufficiently large number of

---

186 Louis Amaya, "Debt as Diversification: Non-Performing Loans (NPLs) and Real Estate Owned (REO) Assets as Alternative Asset Anchors," March 16, 2023, https://www.linkedin.com/pulse/debt-diversification-non-performing-loans-npls-real-estate-amaya/.

investors interpret that the share value of a certain company is going to go up or down, this causes a self-fulfilling prophecy. This can be seen in Gamestop, which had its value increase from $2 billion to over $24 billion in just days.[187]

Here is a formula I like to use to remind people that even with the best fundamental analysis, timing, talent, and effort, which has an exponential impact, luck also plays a role in the final results:

Results = f ((talent ^ effort) × luck)

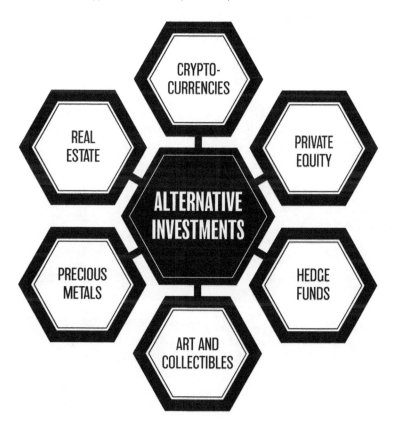

Investing in companies and stocks to make a difference must also provide a return though, because otherwise you won't have the funds

---

187   "The Story of GameStop," Duke University, https://people.duke.edu/~jc910/ HW%201/.

to continue investing and helping. Looking ahead, we can expect to see more and more interest in alternative investments. This is due to both the higher returns that they offer, and also technologies that are making it easier to invest in these kinds of assets. While traditionally only high-net-worth individuals and institutions could participate in alternative investments, there are now ways that more people can get involved. Much of this has to do with tokenization and blockchain, which we'll consider next.

In the meantime, I leave you with a final question to think about: What is the main virtue of an alternative investor? The answer is "patience." Lack of it only benefits your broker.

© Glasbergen/ glasbergen.com

"Do you have any other collateral...
besides this e-mail from a Nigerian prince?"

CHAPTER 17

INVESTING IN RWAS THROUGH TOKENIZATION

As you go along your investment journey, pay careful attention to tokenization, which refers to the process of issuing a digital representation of an asset. Supported by blockchain technology, tokenization is reshaping our world. It's revolutionizing the way we live, work, and interact. It offers transparency, security, and efficiency in our increasingly digital universe. From finance to real estate, and from healthcare to entertainment, tokenization provides a more inclusive and accessible field on which everyone can play.

Due to its growing relevance, we'll spend some time looking at how the technology behind tokenization is disrupting traditional models. We'll also consider the industries using it, and the opportunities it creates, especially for investing in real-world assets (RWAs). While regulation is always part of the development of technology, we can expect to see more tokenization, and opportunities to invest in it, in the coming years.

As you read through the following sections, keep in mind that now is a prime time to learn about tokenization. More people are looking up the term online, as Google indicates. Consider the following graph to see the growing interest in tokenization:

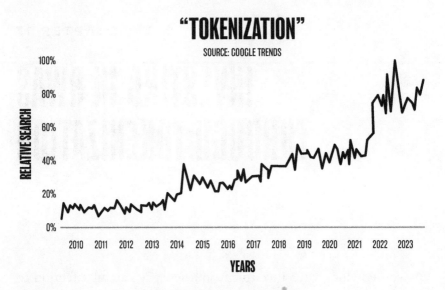

"TOKENIZATION"
SOURCE: GOOGLE TRENDS

THE TECHNOLOGY REVOLUTION

Let's start with the basics. Tokenization is the process of issuing a digital representation of an asset on a blockchain, which is a digital database or ledger distributed among the nodes of a peer-to-peer network.

Blockchain is making its way into a plethora of industries, where it's changing the status quo. The global market for smart contracts, which are programs that automatically run when predetermined conditions are met, is expected to grow at a compound annual growth rate of 82.2 percent between 2023 and 2030.[188]

Blockchain enhances traceability and authenticity in manufacturing, agriculture, and supply chain management, ensuring food safety

---

188 David Pawlan, "Blockchain in FinTech: Exploring Industry Insights 2024," Aloa Blog, https://aloa.co/blog/blockchain-in-fintech.

and reducing fraud. In healthcare, it provides secure patient records, and in education, it makes it easy to safely store and verify academic credentials. For real estate, it offers a digital registry for properties. Media and entertainment industries leverage blockchain for fair copyright payments, helping artists to be compensated in a timely manner. E-commerce companies like Amazon, Alibaba, Nestlé, and Walmart are using blockchain technology to improve transparency across all their processes. The energy industry also benefits from blockchain's decentralized approach, as the technology clearly tracks production and consumption. The legal sector uses blockchain for secure and verifiable records, which helps to protect intellectual property.

Moreover, blockchain has transformative potential in politics and governance. It provides transparent voting systems, as it accurately portrays people's voices. It can record donations and campaign expenses in a public ledger, which reduces the risk of corruption.

OPPORTUNITIES THROUGH TOKENIZATION

Tokenization brings so many new advantages, and there are many ways investors can benefit from these. Now, more people than ever before can make investments that wouldn't have been possible for them in the past. I'm passionate about the opportunities and positive social impact this technology is creating for societies.

Here are a few of the opportunities that tokenization provides:

- *Greater access to assets:* Tokenization removes traditional barriers, allowing smaller investors to get involved in a space that previously was only occupied by large players.
- *Improved liquidity:* Tokenized assets can easily be sold, which gives buyers more flexibility.

- *Markets operate twenty-four hours a day:* This is a very attractive feature for a global audience.
- *Transparency and security:* Blockchain technology records all transactions transparently and in a way that can't be changed. This increases security and trust.
- *Global markets:* Tokenization allows investors from any country in the world to buy tokens of assets located in different regions.
- *Portfolio diversification:* Investors have more alternatives to diversify their portfolios with tokenized assets.
- *Incentives and rewards:* Tokens can be used as part of a reward program, encouraging loyalty and engagement.
- *Alternatives to traditional financing:* Tokenization provides a different option rather than a bank loan or venture capital. Companies, especially small and medium-sized ones, can raise capital quickly without having to go through traditional financing processes.
- *New business models:* Token-based economies allow users to be rewarded for contributing to the platform or ecosystem.
- *Community participation:* Tokens allow groups of people to participate in a project's development and success.

TOKENIZATION AND REAL-WORLD ASSETS

Due to its democratic format and secure setup, tokenization is already being applied to all kinds of assets. This includes RWAs. If you're thinking about investing in tokenized goods, it can be helpful to know what's currently happening in the space.

Here's a look at some of the RWAs that are being tokenized:

- *Art and collections:* By tokenizing artwork and collectibles, artists and collectors can ensure authenticity and track the ownership history. This not only simplifies the process of buying and selling; it also creates opportunities for partial ownership of expensive artwork. With it, art investment is now more accessible.

- *Commodities:* Gold, oil, and agricultural products are being tokenized, which streamlines trading and investment processes. HSBC, one of the largest banks in the world, with over $3 trillion in assets under management, has tokenized gold. Visa has announced the tokenization of agricultural products. There are also curious cases like the tokenization of scarce bottles of wine or barrels of whiskey.

- *Infrastructure and public projects:* Tokenization is being applied to the funding of infrastructure and public projects, including new power plants and public transportation systems. This enables communities to raise funds more efficiently and allows community members to participate in a project that directly benefits them.

- *Intellectual property:* Patents, trademarks, and copyrights can be tokenized, which makes it easier to manage and monetize these assets. Creators and companies can get funding by selling a portion of their intellectual property rights, while still retaining some control over their inventions.

- *Carbon credits and environmental assets:* Tokenization is being used to trade carbon credits and other environmental assets. This incentivizes investment in projects that are beneficial to the environment and contribute to sustainability.

- *Luxury products and collectibles:* High-value items such as watches, cars, and rare collectibles are being tokenized. This makes luxury goods more accessible to a wider audience and creates a new avenue for investment.

- *Sports and entertainment:* Fans can purchase tokens representing a stake in a sports team, music rights, or film projects, allowing them to participate in and benefit from the success of their favorite teams or artists. These tokens can be backed by real activities such as concerts, or image rights of artists or athletes. They can offer unique advantages to token holders, such as access to premium material or participation in team decision-making. The NBA has monetized this new digital era through non-fungible tokens or NFTs, generating over $230 million in revenue to date. Additionally, game developers worldwide are preparing their own tokenization projects and solutions. Mass adoption of GameFi is expected in the coming years.

- *Financial instruments:* Bonds, stocks, and other financial instruments are being tokenized to improve market liquidity and efficiency. Tokenization in this area simplifies the process of buying, selling, and transferring securities, making financial markets more accessible to a wide range of investors. It also reduces the time and cost associated with traditional securities transactions.

- *Debt and loans:* By issuing tokens representing debt, borrowers can access a wider group of investors, while lenders can exchange these tokens, thereby increasing liquidity in this new digital lending market.

- *Real estate:* Thanks to tokenization, a wider range of investors can participate in global real estate markets, diversifying their portfolios without the need for substantial capital, and being able to liquidate their investment at any time. While companies like RealT or Reental continue to add new residential properties to their tokenized offerings, others like Nash21 are converting rental contracts into useful digital assets. Firms like Figure Technologies are working with Goldman Sachs, JPMorgan, and Jefferies Financial Group on a public offering of shares (IPO) for a new blockchain-based digital initiative to originate new lines of credit collateralized with real estate assets, also known as home equity lines of credit (HELOCs).

To see the breakdown of security tokens by industry, consider the following graph:

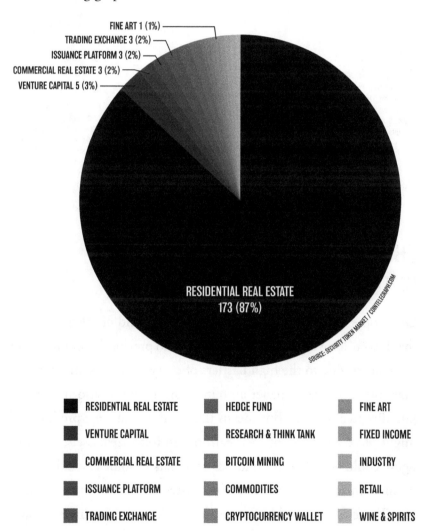

Some of the notable benefits that tokenization brings include the ones highlighted in the following graph:

BENEFITS OF TOKENIZATION

LIQUIDITY	24/7 MARKETS	TRANSACTION COSTS	FRACTIONAL OWNERSHIP
Increases liquidity to asset owners and unlocks new markets.	The blockchain does not sleep. Traditional markets only permit trading in sanctioned hours, whereas the blockchain is a constantly available global technology.	Transaction costs on the Ethereum blockchain are gradually decreasing as scaling capabilities improve.	Instead of only being able to own all-or-none of the asset, blockchain technology allows for fractional ownership making ownership of assets more affordable.
TRANSPARENCY	**FAST SETTLEMENT**	**DeFi**	**BRIDGING THE OLD WITH THE NEW**
The public ledger system creates a public record confirming the existence of a transaction. Anonymity of participants is maintained.	Transactions between various traditional banking institutions take days to settle. International payments can take even longer with flat payments. Blockchain transactions are globally near-instantaneous.	Participating in tokenization gives users access to a broader world of international DeFi technology.	Provides access for traditional finance to inteact with the crypto markets. Tokenization democratize access to ownership of assets. Anyone, anywhere can participate.

THE POWER OF INVESTING IN TOKENIZED ASSETS

One of the largest motivators for me in the world of tokenization is that it is creating access to new investors who previously couldn't enter the market, due to the high barriers of entry. With tokenized assets, investors can invest smaller amounts, and they can also have more liquidity than before. This means that a middle-income professional might place a portion of their earnings in tokenized assets, and this figure could be as low as hundreds of dollars in some cases. They can monitor their investment, and if they need the money, they can cash out. This creates a world of opportunity for beginning investors and opens the door to a future of potentially strong growth. Suddenly a middle-income professional can get returns that were only available to institutional investors and high-net-worth individuals in the past.

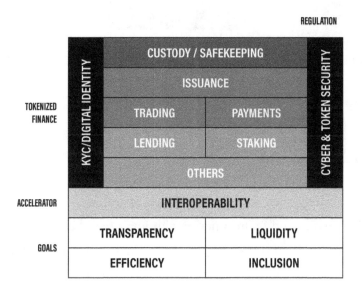

To see this at work, we'll consider the case of Reental, where I am chairman and have invested my time and resources to work toward a cause I am passionate about. Reental is a real estate investment platform and the leader in tokenized assets under management in Europe and Latam. It is also the leader in the Spanish-speaking market, and the company with the fastest growth in the Americas. It focuses on exclusive, high-demand, value-added properties that guarantee a high rental yield and future appreciation.

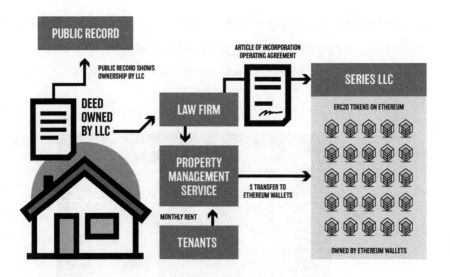

Through Reental, users can invest in real estate in Europe, the United States, and Latin America with just a few clicks. Investors can put in as little as $100 and get an average annual return of more than 14 percent. They also receive monthly passive income streams and 24/7 liquidity, thanks to blockchain and smart contracts. Reental has a community of more than fourteen thousand users from over seventy-five countries as I write this. When people invest with Reental, nine out of ten choose to reinvest. In fact, during a recent equity funding round, more than 50 percent of the sources came from the platform's users.

At Reental, users can automatically reinvest their earnings. This can provide benefits such as tax deferral. It also leads to compound interest and the chance to keep growing their investment quickly.

Considerations	Reental	Real Estate	Stocks	Digital Assets	Gold	Bonds	CDs
Attractive Yield	✓	✓	✓	✓	✓	✓	✗
Volatility	Low	Low	High	Extreme	Low	Low	Low
Risk Level	Low	Low	High	Extreme	Low	Low	Low
Accessibility	✓	✗	✓	✗	✗	✗	✗
24/7 Liquidity	✓	✗	✗	✗	✗	✗	✗
Tangible Asset	✓	✓	✗	✗	✓	✗	✗
Inflation Hedge	✓	✓	✓	✓	✓	✗	✗
Annual Return	13-30%	7-14%	10-20%	Highly Variable	8-12%	10-12%	2-6%

Now at Reental, we are focused on expansion, which will further help users to upgrade their money. We anticipate increasing demand trends that are related to the relocation of large companies to certain areas of opportunity, sociodemographic or zoning changes, and tourism reforms, among others. We add value to properties and renovate them, if necessary, based on the demand drivers in a location. We might create spaces that offer coliving options for renters, coworking spaces, short- or long-term residential rentals, room rentals, and vacation rentals, among others. For instance, Reental has tokenized the first coliving space in the world located in Malaga, Spain, and also the first cave house with a private natural hot spring pool, situated in San Miguel de Allende in Mexico.

For small- and medium-sized investors, the lower barriers to entry are a welcome relief. Digitizing real estate assets means that their value can be fractionalized. This provides greater levels of access to global capital and allows international investors to participate. The transfers are also faster and cheaper, making it more efficient and less costly for investors.

Tokenization can also be used by real estate owners and developers to obtain financing, which reduces their dependence on bank loans. Blockchain technology can also improve property management, which creates a more streamlined property tracking and management system.

REGULATIONS AND TOKENIZATION

Obviously, compliance with local regulations is essential for tokenizing assets and selling tokens. Requirements vary depending on different jurisdictions. However, it is common in all of them for token issuers to comply with Anti-Money Laundering (AML) and Know Your Customer (KYC) rules. Look for orderly procedures when investing and be wary if you don't see a sign of compliance.

New regulations, such as the Markets in Crypto Assets (MiCA) in Europe, will increase awareness and confidence in blockchain technology and tokenization. There are also evolving regulatory frameworks around the world, especially in places such as Singapore, the United Kingdom, Japan, and Abu Dhabi.

In the case of Reental, the firm complies with the regulations and validation standards of the CNMV (Comisión Nacional del Mercado de Valores) in Spain, and it also follows the regulations required by the SEC in the United States.

To see how tokenization is taking off, consider the following graph:

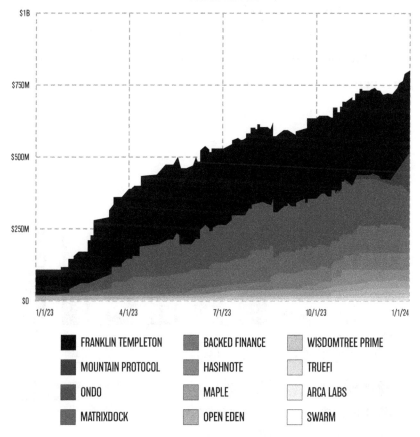

TOKENIZED U.S. TREASURY PRODUCT MARKET CAPS
SOURCE: RWA.XYZ

Legend:
- FRANKLIN TEMPLETON
- MOUNTAIN PROTOCOL
- ONDO
- MATRIXDOCK
- BACKED FINANCE
- HASHNOTE
- MAPLE
- OPEN EDEN
- WISDOMTREE PRIME
- TRUEFI
- ARCA LABS
- SWARM

You might be asking, "What's next for tokenization?" I believe there are two dimensions to each RWA. Every asset that can be tokenized is a combination of both dimensions and faces different challenges based on where it sits on the spectrum. I am convinced that opportunities for tokenization exist for all tangible and intangible assets, along with all real and financial assets.

Tokenization is estimated to have a market of $16 trillion by 2030 according to BCG, as we can see in the following graph.[189] This would be 10 percent of global GDP. Given this, we have only just begun to see its potential. This is in line with Roland Berger's projections, who believes that we will reach these figures if we tokenize even just 1 percent of the RWA market.[190]

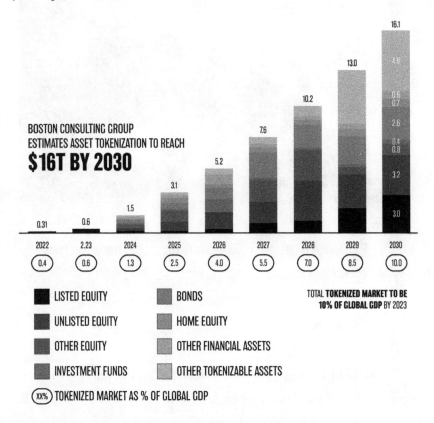

---

189 Martin Young, "Real-World Asset Tokenization Could Surge to $16t Industry by 2030," Crypto Potato, April 2, 2023, https://cryptopotato.com/real-world-asset-tokenization-could-surge-to-16t-industry-by-2030-research/#:~:text=Research%20by%20the%20Boston%20Consulting,and%20silver%20and%20real%20estate.

190 Roland Berger, "Tokenization of Real-World Assets," Roland Berger, https://www.rolandberger.com/en/Insights/Publications/Tokenization-of-real-world-assets-unlocking-a-new-era-of-ownership-trading.html.

In case you have any doubts left after reading this about tokeni-zation, I encourage you to reflect on Larry Fink, CEO of Blackrock, the world's largest asset management company. Blackrock owns more than 85 percent of the shares in the S&P 500. Fink has become a staunch media evangelist for tokenization.[191] He considers it to be the cornerstone of a new, more efficient, sustainable, and inclusive financial sector.

---

191 Shanny Basar, "Fund Tokenization on the Rise," Markets Media, January 24, 2024, https://www.marketsmedia.com/fund-tokenization-on-the-riseD.

© Glasbergen/ glasbergen.com

"You have been approved for a fixed-rate mortgage.
That means if interest rates go up again and
you're not paying enough, we'll fix it."

CHAPTER 18

THE CHANGING WORLD THROUGH DEFI

As we continue our discussion on investments, it's worth pointing out the increasing adoption of a new way to transact, known as DeFi. This refers to a financial system that is built on blockchain technology. Unlike traditional finance methods, which rely on centralized parties like banks and exchanges to facilitate transactions, DeFi operates on decentralized networks. It uses smart contracts to automate processes and doesn't need a third party like a bank to carry out a transaction.

With more organizations and individuals taking DeFi seriously, changes have taken place—and many more will come. To make the most of your money, you'll want to be aware of what's going on, and how you can get involved too. We'll spend some time looking at how DeFi is breaking into the financial services industry. We'll consider its potential implications, and what you need to know about it to make smarter investments.

A SHIFT FOR FINANCIAL SERVICES

Traditionally, if you wanted to take out a loan or access funds, you would have to go through a financial institution such as a bank. Under this arrangement, many people found themselves left out. They might not be able to pay the fees involved or meet the needed requirements to borrow money. The barriers to entry for investing, too, have typically been high. Without a large enough net worth, it wouldn't be possible to invest in certain assets with the potential for higher returns.

DeFi changes all of that suddenly, anyone with an internet connection and a digital wallet can get involved. DeFi essentially eliminates the intermediaries who were once involved and makes it possible to exchange in a peer-to-peer way. The way that money moves could soon be very different, especially as blockchain and digital assets become more present in the mainstream market. According to content by Deloitte, cryptocurrencies, stablecoins, and tokenized assets, which all can be programmed, are replacing services that once were carried out by banks, stock exchanges, and brokers.[192]

DeFi provides greater access to consumers around the world. If people have internet access or a smartphone, they may be able to participate in the financial system. They might not have a bank account, but they'll be able to transact through digital forms of currency that are supported by blockchain. In the same way, companies and even governments can exchange and interact in new ways through DeFi.

---

192 "Decentralized Finance May Transform How Money Is Managed," Deloitte, https://deloitte.wsj.com/cfo/ decentralized-finance-may-transform-how-money-is-managed-7dda94b3.

BRANDS ARE GETTING ON BOARD

A growing number of major banks and banking networks, card networks, and technology providers are getting involved with block-chain networks. Notably, PayPal has just adopted cryptocurrency on its platform, making it accessible to its users. If you have a PayPal account, you can now buy, hold, and sell common cryptocurrencies. You can also cash it out and transfer it between eligible PayPal and Venmo accounts, along with other wallets and exchanges.[193]

PayPal is not alone in this movement toward bringing cryp-tocurrencies and DeFi to the masses. JPMorgan has launched the JPM Coin System, a blockchain-based account ledger and payment system. It has also created Onyx Digital Assets, which is a tokenization platform that allows financial institutions and others to record and represent financial assets as programmable tokens on a blockchain. For investors, JPMorgan and Apollo Global Management are looking to create a portfolio management system that is powered by blockchain, smart contracts, and tokenization.[194]

Goldman Sachs is investing in DeFi and preparing for change, too. The firm has moved into trading in cryptocurrencies and has launched its own digital asset platform. It joined Canton, which is a blockchain network that provides connections between organizations through smart contracts. S&P Global, Moody's, Broadbridge, and Capgemini have also gotten involved in Canton. The idea is to have a place where both data and value can be safely exchanged.

---

193 Ibid.

194 Ibid.

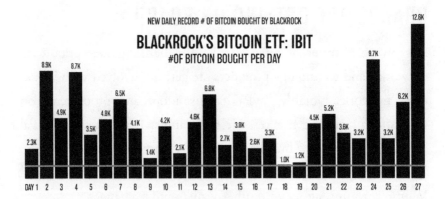

REGULATION IS INCREASING

Often when innovation takes place, there are no regulations to monitor it at first. As industries are disrupted, the governing bodies look for ways to set limits and provide a layer of protection for users. Once regulation begins, it's often a sign that the new technologies are being adopted and will become more common in the future.

For DeFi, many countries are looking into regulatory frameworks to allow the use of digital assets. About 130 jurisdictions around the world are launching, piloting, developing, or researching central bank digital currencies. California also implemented two bills: one for virtual currency licensing and another to regulate digital financial asset transactions. The SEC in the United States approved the listing and trading of several spot bitcoin-exchange traded funds, making it easier to invest in bitcoin. The Financial Accounting Standards Board has created guidelines for cryptocurrency and other digital assets. Even the IRS has developed guidance on digital assets and is treating them as property for federal tax purposes.[195]

---

195   Ibid.

Through DeFi, everything from supply chains to payroll could be managed differently. Governments might oversee global treasuries in a different way. The methods used to collect taxes and manage investment accounts could change as well.

DAILY ETF SPOT BITCOIN HITS $10B

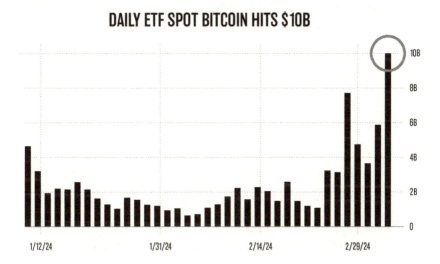

THE ADVANTAGES OF DEFI

What's drawing so many people to cryptocurrencies and blockchain? Why are governments looking for ways to set guidelines for new transactions? What is making large financial institutions get involved in tokenization?

Certainly, when cryptocurrencies were first talked about, and entered the market, there were steep highs and lows. Over time, with the advancement of technology, more are beginning to see the potential for digital assets and blockchain. This way of transacting provides many benefits compared to the traditional methods for financing.

Here are some of the advantages that DeFi brings that investors will want to know about:

- *Greater transparency:* Blockchain technology, which forms the backbone of DeFi, enables secure transactions without the need for intermediaries. With smart contracts, financial processes can be automated. This includes lending, borrowing, and trading. All of this helps to streamline the transaction and reduce risk.

- *Financial inclusion:* DeFi has the potential to create greater access for the world's population to financial services. This includes those who don't have a bank account. With just a smartphone and internet connection, individuals can access DeFi platforms to make investments and earn interest on their assets. They can participate in investment opportunities that weren't available to them in the past.

- *Global access:* Since DeFi operates on open, permissionless networks, anyone who has an internet connection can get involved. This makes it easier to carry out transactions across borders and encourages international trade. You can be in control of your finances, regardless of where you live.

- *Community accountability:* Many DeFi protocols are governed by decentralized autonomous organizations (DAOs). Through these, token holders collectively make decisions about the platform's governance, protocol upgrades, and how resources are allocated. Community-driven accountability helps ensure that DeFi platforms adapt to the needs of their users.

As we look into the coming years, we can expect that DeFi will continue to move into the mainstream. Consumers around the world will be able to enjoy financial products and services in ways that weren't possible in the past. Individuals will be able to invest and make decisions about their future.

The positive impact that DeFi is making is what excites me most. I see the chance for alternative investments to be made, no matter where you are or what you earn. By getting involved, we can help people take charge of building their own wealth on their own terms. With lower risk and greater opportunities for returns, the future is bright. If you haven't gotten involved in DeFi, it may be time to start thinking about it.

DEFI'S TVL $100B NEW RECORD

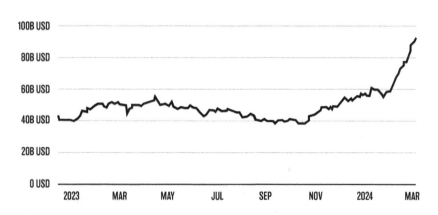

© Glasbergen/ glasbergen.com

"My financial strategy? Hope for the best, but plan for the worst."

CHAPTER 19

MANAGING AI AND ML INVESTING

Today, as we've seen, picking out investments takes time and research, and you often need to look carefully to see if a company is helping to make a positive social impact. There are so many options available that it may seem difficult to get started. As you compare different investments, you'll want to think about long-term results, their future value, and many of the strategies we have covered up to now to increase your chances of a higher return, minimizing your risks and downside.

When you carry out investigations, keep in mind that there are tools that can enable us to make smarter decisions, and many of these are related to technology. With recent advancements, AI and ML are able to manage large amounts of data and provide insights that we might otherwise overlook. Nowadays, 98 percent of financial advisors consider AI to be a pivotal tool that is reshaping how advice is formed, delivered, and consumed by clients.[196]

This digital assistance could be useful as you make decisions. A good starting point is to understand their potential, as they are transforming the way people manage their finances. As in any other industry, there's going to be an AI copilot for every profession you can think of, to help that person do their job, so you'll also want to know how investing advisors that you work with are implementing these technologies.

In the following sections, I'll share the advantages AI and ML are providing for the industry. I'll also explain how we, at Savia Capital, are using them, along with other strategies, to make smarter investment decisions. As you read, you'll see that it's not just a case of learning about new tools. It's much more than that; AI and ML are disrupting the traditional investment approaches, and to upgrade your own money, it is critical to know what they can do to help you avoid losses and increase your smarter alternative investments returns.

AI AND ML IN TOKENIZATION

AI and ML are increasingly being integrated into asset tokenization. This means the technology can be used to optimize investment strategies, oversee risk management, and make informed decisions. AI and ML analyze vast amounts of data to find patterns, predict market trends, and identify the perceived and real value of tokenized assets.

See the following graph to see the emerging technologies that are impacting asset tokenization:

---

196 "More Financial Advisors Turning to AI Tools for Clients, Survey Shows," Wisconsin Institute of Certified Public Accountants, August 5, 2022, https://www.wicpa.org/news/articles/1750:more-financial-advisors-turning-to-ai-tools-for-clients-survey-shows.

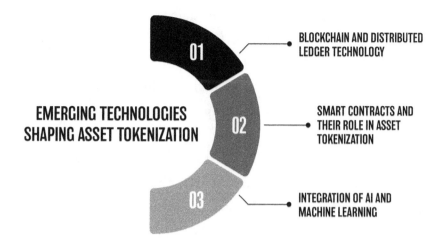

PUTTING AI AND ML INTO PRACTICE

At Savia Capital, we use several practices to make smarter investment decisions. We look at our fundamental analysts' insights as a starting point. We also draw on crowd wisdom, to see what others collectively are saying about a company or asset. Finally, we use AI and ML to help us compare the options and see which ones stand out as winners.

Our investment strategy allows us to analyze the companies or assets using the traditional value investing approach, along with the public sentiment about them. AI and ML systems allow us to identify correlations, patterns, and rankings that are continually updated. This provides clear comparative insights, and since AI doesn't have feelings, it is not affected by traditional investor emotions. There's no need to worry about AI being fearful or greedy, and it doesn't struggle with reactionary behaviors during recessions, economic crises, or market crashes. Instead, it helps us to drive more informed, accurate, and speedy decision-making. This ultimately leads to better investing results or alpha (alpha measures an investment's excess return, aka performance, compared to a benchmark index or the market, while beta measures an investment's volatility compared to the overall market).

To see how this all works and the difference it can make, a good example is FINQ Stocks Products (finquai.com). This platform offers stock portfolios that are built to outperform the market and uses AI to make smarter investment decisions. Its products are based on a full ranking of all S&P stocks, which are generated every day by tools that analyze millions of data points from multiple sources. Its AI-powered engine gathers insight from investment experts and Wall Street analysts, media and social media traffic and trends, and company-specific information. With this strategy, it has been able to provide higher returns than the S&P 500. For instance, in February 2024, while S&P 500 provided a return of 21.18 percent, FINQFIRST gained 59.27 percent, nearly three times as much as the S&P 500.[197]

As you can see, there is significant potential for investing with AI and ML. The returns could be greater, as you're able to take advantage of tools that can process massive amounts of data and keep continual track of companies. If you're getting started in investing, I encourage you to think about how AI and ML could be used in your own strategy. If you don't apply it personally, you might consider working with someone who understands its potential and knows how to maximize the technology.

40 YEARS IN ONE SLIDE: SAVIA CAPITAL
Smarter Alternative Value-Investing Fund **RE (REO&NPL) + PE (BC&AI) + HNW (ART&DA)**

INVESTMENT PHILOSOPHY:	
· PRIME INFO & ASSETS ACCESS	· FUNDAMENTAL ANALYSIS & VA
· MULTI-BAGGERS & COMPOUNDERS	· TOKENIZATION & DEFI
· SKIN IN THE GAME & SECONDARIES	· BIG DATA & AI/ML
· ASYMMETRIC & UNCORRELATED INVS	

---

197 "FINQ Stocks Products," FINQ Stocks, https://finqai.com/stocks/portfolios.

PART 3

UPGRADE YOUR LEGACY

© Glasbergen/ glasbergen.com

"If Robin Hood takes from the rich and gives it to the poor,
then eventually *everyone* will be poor. Explain to me
again why that makes him a hero?"

CHAPTER 20

THE CHANCE TO MAKE A DIFFERENCE

When I look back on my career and business developments, I am most proud of the opportunities I have had to improve the lives of others. I believe creating educational access can help societies move in the right direction. I also want to see individuals who didn't always have a chance to invest be given a way to upgrade their money. These days, I mentor others and am always ready to answer questions that might help others who are trying to upgrade their lives.

For education, I found ways to provide funds for scholarships to students who otherwise might not be able to continue going to school. If you have limited funding, the doors for learning can close, especially in university settings. However, when given a chance to study, individuals can acquire the resilience needed to work toward a degree, which can lead to better habits, paying jobs, and a satisfying career.

In addition, I'm an advocate for families throughout Latin America and beyond. At Reental, we are making investing accessible to everyone with just one click. They can invest starting at $100, and get an internal rate of return of more than 13 percent with 24/7 liquidity if they need it. We are also the first company in the world to provide features as a peer-to-peer marketplace, automatic monthly passive income thanks to the smart contracts, collateralized loans thanks to DeFi with non-volatile RWA tokens as collateral, along with the option to invest in smart housing, smart cities, smart renting, or very soon in real estate tokenized index funds.

For mentoring, I am always happy to connect with others looking to learn more about how to make a smarter use of their savings or build smarter portfolios. I hope that this book can become a resource for all of you who are beginning in this exciting world of alternative investments.

When you are working to make a difference in the lives of others, you will often find satisfaction in your work. A sense of fulfillment can help you get through the difficult days. And the good days may seem brighter.

The decisions you make every day, as you invest, can have a lasting impact, even if it's not obvious right away. For example, many millennial investors today are asking about the carbon footprint before they make a choice. When looking at a new car, they might ask about its emissions rather than checking on its engine size or top speed. The Green Deal encourages new trends and a transition to energy-saving improvements, and you could be part of such a movement that brings new sources of incomes and returns while also helping to better the air we breathe every day.

In the following sections, I'll share some quotes on happiness and compassion. As you read them, think about your own life and purpose. Consider if you've found ways to make a difference, or if you're still searching for the right path.

HAPPINESS AND COMPASSION

HAPPINESS LIES IN THE JOY OF ACHIEVEMENT

Aldous Huxley used to say that happiness is generally the by-product of other activities.[198] In fact, according to Lyubomirsky, Sheldon, and Schkade's research, our happiness is based on the following: 50 percent genes, 10 percent circumstances, and 40 percent intentional activity.[199] It is consequently our responsibility to create it. According to Harvard research, achieving positive relationships keeps us happier, healthier, and helps us to live longer.[200]

BUILD YOUR HAPPINESS ON THE RIGHT PILLARS

Becoming a happy person doesn't depend on having the perfect family, job, or lifestyle. In fact, it doesn't depend on having the perfect anything. To be happy, you must take responsibility for your life and your actions. Simply, cultivate deep and meaningful relationships with your family and friends, find a job or business that is satisfying in terms of your skills and supportive colleagues, and be part of something that inspires awe and wonder.

---

198 Aldous Huxley, "Aldous Huxley Quotes," Goodreads.com https://www.goodreads.com/author/quotes/3487.Aldous_Huxley.

199 Kira Newman, "How Much of Your Happiness Is under Your Control?" Greater Good Magazine, February 18, 2020, https://greatergood.berkeley.edu/article/item/how_much_of_your_happiness_is_under_your_control.

200 Marc Schulz, "An 85-Year Harvard Study Found the No. 1 Thing That Makes Us Happy in Life: It Helps Us 'Live Longer,'" CNBC, February 10, 2023, https://www.cnbc.com/2023/02/10/85-year-harvard-study-found-the-secret-to-a-long-happy-and-successful-life.html.

THERE IS NO WAY TO HAPPINESS— HAPPINESS IS THE WAY

William Saroyan stated that "The greatest happiness you can have is knowing that you do not necessarily require happiness."[201] And remember Lao Tzu's wisdom: "If you are not happy with little, you will not be happy with much."[202] I also recommend following the Stoics in balancing a eudaimonic happiness (feeling good contributing to others) with a hedonic one (seasoning life with moments of pleasure from time to time).

LOOK FOR AREAS WHERE YOU CAN REALLY IMPROVE

As Jim Rohn stated, "Your life does not get better by chance; it gets better by change."[203] And keep in mind that dreams do not come true at the snap of a finger. They require patience and determination.

FOCUS ON WHAT BRINGS FULFILLMENT

As Steve Jobs said, "The only way to do great work is to love what you do."[204]

---

201 William Saroyan, "William Saroyan Quotes," Goodreads.com, https://www.goodreads.com/quotes/183013-the-greatest-happiness-you-can-have-is-knowing-that-you.

202 "The 35 Best Quotes by Lao Tse, the Father of Taoism," Step to Health, https://step-tohealth.com/the-35-best-quotes-by-lao-tse-the-father-of-taoism/.

203 Jim Rohn, "Jim Rohn Quotes," Goodreads.com, https://www.goodreads.com/quotes/561636-your-life-does-not-get-better-by-chance-it-gets.

204 Steve Jobs, "Steve Jobs Quotes," Goodreads.com, https://www.goodreads.com/quotes/772887-the-only-way-to-do-great-work-is-to-love.

REMEMBER YOU CAN'T BUY EVERYTHING

As Naval Ravikant stated, "A fit body, a calm mind, a house full of love. These things cannot be bought—they must be earned."[205]

TIP AS IF YOU WERE THE TIPPEE

All of us are tippers. And today's tippee might be your tipper tomorrow.

PRACTICE SISU

"Sisu" is a way of living in Finland, known as the happiest country in the world.[206] Basically, it consists of finding a greater purpose to connect with, increasing resilience through training, being gentle with yourself and others, and connecting with nature regularly. Get quiet, enjoy the wonders of nature, listen to birds, and smell the grass and flowers.

ENJOY WHAT YOU DO

It is not that we bite off more than we can chew; it's that we bite off more than we can savor.

I think it was Francisco de Ayala who said at 101 years of age, "Happiness is doing what you think you should do and doing it with pleasure."

---

205 Naval Ravikant, "Naval Ravikant Quotes," Goodreads.com, https://www.goodreads. com/quotes/9221707-a-fit-body-a-calm-mind-a-house-full-of.

206 E. Elisabet Lahti, "Finland Is Home to the World's Happiest People. Their No. 1 Secret Is This 500-Year-Old Mindset, Says Psychology Expert," June 30, 2023, https://www. cnbc.com/2023/06/30/im-a-psychologist-in-finland-this-500-year-old-mindset-makes-us-the-worlds-happiest-people.html.

FOLLOW THE RIGHT PATH

As St. Augustine of Hippo shared, "Wrong is wrong, even if everyone is doing it. Right is right, even if no one is doing it."[207] And as Roy T. Bennett shared, "Do what is right, not what is easy nor what is popular."[208] Elon Musk added, "When something is important enough, you do it even if the odds are not in your favor."[209]

BEAUTY DOESN'T GUARANTEE HAPPINESS

From time to time, I read or listen to young people referring to those wonderful models or Instagram influencers as examples to emulate to achieve "their happiness." Just like material possessions, beauty or being a makeup/photoshop expert does not make a person happier. Of course, it can improve your self-esteem, but generally only for a while. Belief that we are already beautiful, without any external assistance, is the critical improvement our minds need.

IN THE FACE OF FLATTERY AND INSULT, BE LIKE A FICUS TREE

Known as a symbol for peace, the Ficus tree (commonly called the fig tree) is a good attitude to convey. Anger is self-destructive and does not bring us any benefit.

---

207 St. Augustine, "St. Augustine Quotes," Goodreads.com, https://www.goodreads.com/quotes/126110-right-is-right-even-if-no-one-is-doing-it.

208 Roy T. Bennett, "Roy T. Bennett Quotes," Goodreads.com, https://www.goodreads.com/quotes/7858741-do-what-is-right-not-what-is-easy-nor-what.

209 Elon Musk, "Elon Musk Quotes," BrainyQuote.com, https://www.brainyquote.com/quotes/elon_musk_567219.

HAPPINESS IS ABOUT GIVING, NOT JUST RECEIVING

If you try to get enough of something to be happy, you will never be happy.

BE GRATEFUL

Grateful people are happier, more energetic, more helpful, and experience more frequent positive emotions. So, every time you brush your teeth, review what good things have happened since your last tooth brushing session.

BE A HUGGER

Hugs are free and serve as pain relievers and antidepressants. Hugging is not only a token of love but also helps us to relieve stress, diminish pain, and make us feel much closer to others. I consider a true hug to be "heart to heart," and to be held for at least three seconds. According to research from Carnegie Mellon University, huggers become much happier, so be a hugger please.[210]

BE OPTIMISTIC

Optimism requires persistence and determination. Optimistic people tend to interpret their troubles as temporary, controllable, and specific to one situation. Pessimistic people, in contrast, believe that their troubles are permanent, uncontrollable, and undermine everything they do. Whenever you face adversity, listen carefully to your explanations for it. If these explanations are pessimistic, actively challenge them. Pessimistic labels lead to passivity, whereas optimistic ones lead to attempts to change. Use evidence, alternatives, and usefulness when

---

210 "Hug It Out: Study Shows Hugs Really Do Make Us Happier, Especially on Hard Days," StudyFinds.com, October 4, 2018, https://studyfinds.org/study-hugs-happier-harder-days/.

challenging your explanations. We not only need to be optimistic to fight depression, get a promotion, or become a leader (remember others are more drawn to optimistic people), but to give a sense of hope to those around us. There is evidence that optimistic people have a higher quality of life.[211]

WHEN GIVING TO CHARITY, REMEMBER THE LAW OF DIMINISHING RETURNS

Charitable giving, like most other economic endeavors, is subject to the law of diminishing returns, which states that the more of something you add, the less of a difference each new addition makes. To illustrate this, imagine that you've become homeless. One sweater might protect you from hypothermia, but if you already have numerous sweaters, then an additional sweater will make very little difference to your quality of life. The same thing applies to charitable donations, where each additional dollar makes less of a difference than the last. So spread out your contributions wisely.

BE READY TO ACT

According to Mahatma Gandhi, "You may never know what results come of your actions, but if you do nothing, there will be no results."[212] And H. Jackson Brown Jr. added, "Twenty years from now you will

---

211 Matthew Haney and Alvin Wong, "Is Optimism Associated with Increased Quality of Life and Life-Expectancy in Adult Patients?" *Evidence-Based Practice* 25, no. 5 (May 2022): 39–40, https://journals.lww.com/ebp/citation/2022/05000/is_optimism_associated_with_increased_quality_of.31.aspx.

212 Mahatma Gandhi, "Mahatma Gandhi Quotes," Goodreads.com, https://www.goodreads.com/quotes/3343-you-may-never-know-what-results-come-of-your-actions.

be more disappointed by the things that you didn't do than by the ones you did do."[213]

BE FORGIVING

Forgiveness is the answer to almost everything. When we are stuck, it usually means there is more forgiveness to be done. When we are not flowing freely with life in the present moment, it usually means we are holding on to a past moment. It can be regret, sadness, hurt, fear, guilt, blame, anger, resentment, or sometimes even a desire for revenge. We need to release every bit of resentment to make room for change. As Pamela Short stated, "The best revenge is none. Heal, move on and don't become like those who hurt you."[214]

BE FREE FROM THE CONTROL OF OTHERS

Don't let yourself be controlled by any of the following three things: people, money, or past experiences.

LIVE EACH DAY TO THE FULLEST

Life will not postpone your death. So do not postpone your life. As Buddha stated, "One moment can change a day, one day can change a life and one life can change the world."[215]

---

213 H. Jackson Brown Jr., "H. Jackson Brown Jr. Quotes," Goodreads.com, https://www.goodreads.com/ quotes/2340-twenty-years-from-now-you-will-be-more-disappointed-by.

214 Pamela Short, "Pamela Short Quotes," Goodreads.com, https://www.goodreads. com/quotes/11585241-the-best-revenge-is-none-heal-move-on-and-don-t.

215 Buddha, "Buddha Quotes," Goodreads.com, https://www.goodreads.com/ quotes/603942-one-moment-can-change-a-day-one-day-can-change.

KEEP TO YOURSELF WHEN APPROPRIATE

Khalil Gibran stated, "Travel and tell no one, live a true love story and tell no one, live happily and tell no one. People ruin beautiful things."[216]

IDENTIFY YOUR FAVORITE BOOK, SONG, AND MOVIE (AND RENEW THEM FROM TIME TO TIME)

It makes you more aware of the pleasurable experiences that life provides. My current favorite book is *A Christmas Carol*, as it is a great story that reminds us, year after year, of the reason to love and cherish each other and be grateful for the smallest things. The song I like most is "I Will Always Love You," as the singer Whitney Houston has a beautiful voice, and the message is essential. My favorite movie is *Schindler's List* for its most impressive example of how you can impact the world being an entrepreneur.

"I AM HAPPY BECAUSE I WANT NOTHING FROM ANYONE"[217]

Albert Einstein is attributed to saying this, and I believe it's a great quote that deserves daily reflection.

COMPASSION IS BETWEEN EQUALS

The word compassion comes from the Latin words for "suffering together." As Pema Chödrön said, "It is not a relationship between

---

216   Kahlil Gibran, "Kahlil Gibran Quotes," Goodreads.com, https://www.goodreads.com/quotes/7839456-travel-and-tell-no-one-live-a-true-love-story.

217   Albert Einstein, "Albert Einstein Quotes," QuoteFancy.com, https://quotefancy.com/quote/763440/Albert-Einstein-I-am-happy-because-I-want-nothing-from-anyone-I-do-not-care-for-money.

the healer and the wounded. It's a relationship between equals."[218] And as the Dalai Lama stressed, "Compassion and happiness are not a sign of weakness but a sign of strength."[219]

As you go about your day and week, consider that compassion and happiness can be found in simple ways. It may mean simply smiling or helping one person with one task. Or it could mean investing in a company that is working to create social change. You might even start your own business that aligns with ways that you miss or want to make a difference.

---

218 Pema Chödrön, "Pema Chödrön Quotes," Goodreads.com, https://www.goodreads.com/quotes/179969-compassion-is-not-a-relationship-between-the-healer-and-the.

219 Dalai Lama, "Dalai Lama Quotes," Glasp.co, https://glasp.co/quotes/dalai-lama.

© Glasbergen/ glasbergen.com

"I'm looking for a mentor who will show me how to get rich without boring me with a lot of advice."

CHAPTER 21

THE DEFINITION OF LASTING WEALTH

Experts define wealth in many ways. Some place a figure next to it, indicating you have to reach a certain level in income or net worth to be rich.

I don't place a number next to wealth. Throughout this book, I have spent time explaining ways to upgrade your life, your money, and your legacy. Part of your wealth will include the relationships you have in your life and the impact you make in the life of others, directly or indirectly. Take time to identify how you can make the most positive impact with your talents and strengths, but also to be around your loved ones and enjoy their company. Another aspect of it involves your free time. Make sure you are doing things on a daily basis that you enjoy and that help you feel calm. There is an aspect related to finances too. As I've pointed out, investing in yourself, in your business, in other companies, and in alternative assets can all help increase your income and your most valuable asset, your time.

The key, of course, is to take action in the right way. I would advise you to look at your life as a continual learning journey. What I first experienced as a child, and later as an adult, have all helped shape the person I am today. You'll find that, too. Don't be discouraged by handicaps and failures along the way. Remember they are stepping stones to move you toward a higher and better goal.

In closing this book, I leave you with some quotes and inspiration on building lasting wealth. As you go over these, remember that it is more than a numbers game. Overall, you'll want to strive for unbalanced harmony, good relationships, a persistent attitude or grit, and goals that motivate you. Oh, and remember to smile, to be kind, and to take time to laugh and enjoy the small moments along the way.

BUILDING LASTING WEALTH

SPEND RESPONSIBLY

Plan ahead, budget accordingly, avoid unnecessary temptations, and don't buy things just because they are on sale. Charlie Munger also put it in this way: "It's so simple. You spend less than you earn. Invest shrewdly, and avoid toxic people and toxic activities, and try and keep learning all your life, and do a lot of deferred gratification. If you do all those things, you are almost certain to succeed. And if you don't, you're going to need a lot of luck."[220]

---

220 Grace Meyer, "Charlie Munger's 'Great Lesson' of Life: Cut Out Toxic People," Yahoo!Finance, https://finance.yahoo.com/news/ billionaires-top-advice-success-cut-171159263.

YOUR NETWORK IS YOUR NET WORTH

Your social connections are the best investments you can make.

USE LEVERAGE ONLY AS MUCH AS NECESSARY

There is no such thing as a 100 percent sure thing in investing. That is why the use of leverage is dangerous. Use it sparingly and only when you have legitimate inside information.

ADMIRE AND STUDY OTHER RICH PEOPLE

The average person usually resents rich people and avoids learning from them. Instead of being average, follow in the footsteps of successful people. Charlie Munger's formula for success, mentioned previously in this chapter, can be paraphrased as follows: Spend less than you earn, invest prudently, avoid toxic people and toxic activities, defer gratification, and never stop learning.

SUCCESS BEGETS SUCCESS

Associate with positive and successful people, and fully believe you are every bit as good as them. Personal relationships are probably the most underestimated success factor.

FIND PLEASURE IN THE DAY TO DAY

As Robin Sharma advised, "Read more books. Walk in nature daily. Let go of the past. Drink more water. Say thank you a lot. Get up at 5 a.m. Smile at strangers. Meditate. Keep a journal."[221]

---

221 Robin Sharma, "Library Mindset," https://twitter.com/librarymindset/status/16214761
06598760448?lang=en.

TAKE A SHOWER

If you need to relax or have good ideas, enjoy the loneliness and lack of distractions of a good warm shower.

GET PAID BASED ON RESULTS

Most people choose to get paid based on time. You'll learn and get more by asking to be compensated based on results.

FOCUS ON LEARNING AND ACQUIRING EXPERIENCE, AND MONEY WILL FOLLOW

And if money does not follow or you lose it, remember what Sam Walton or someone else said on the day he lost $100 million: "It's just money."

GET COMFORTABLE WITH BEING UNCOMFORTABLE

By expanding your comfort zone, you will expand your wealth zone. You can predict someone's success in any area just by observing how they deal with uncomfortable conversations. Your personal progression is trapped behind uncomfortable conversations.

PLAY TO WIN VERSUS TO NOT LOSE

This mindset will impact your overall performance in life, including sports, business, and personal goals. Playing small does not serve the world. In fact, we win or we learn, but we never lose. You'll win more if you look for ways to make others win—this is especially true when building new businesses.

THINK "BOTH" VERSUS "EITHER/OR"

This is a more inclusive approach to problem-solving and decision-making, enabling you to tap into a broader range of possibilities.

THINK IN TERMS OF ASSETS, NOT INCOME

Wealthy people are not smarter, luckier, or greedier than anyone else. They simply view money as an asset, not as income, that can grow into more money over time.

IF THESE THREE THINGS ARE OVERUSED, THEY CAN RUIN YOUR LIFE: POWER, SEX, AND GREED

The insatiable hunger for wealth, driven by unbridled greed, can lead individuals down a path of moral decay and spiritual impoverishment, corroding the very fabric of their existence.

BETTER THAN RICH, CONSIDER BECOME A "FRILLIONAIRE"—THAT IS, A "FREEDOM MILLIONAIRE"

Extreme materialism and managing properties that are not necessary steal a lot of time. As Bill Gates answered in an interview, "I can understand having millions of dollars. There's meaningful freedom that comes with that, but once you get much beyond that, I have to tell you, it's the same hamburger."[222]

IT'S NOT WHAT YOU HAVE OR DO; IT'S WHO YOU ARE

And you are what you do with what you have, and what you do depends on how you feel about what you know (a nice and wise unexpected play on words ;)).

---

222 Chris Matyszczyk, "Bill Gates: Being Very Rich Is 'The Same Hamburger,'" CNET, October 28, 2011, https://www.cnet.com/culture/bill-gates-being-very-rich-is-the-same-hamburger/.

TO FEEL RICH IS NOT AN EXPERIENCE BUT A DECISION

As Coco Chanel used to say, "There are people who have money and people who are rich."[223] If you want wealth, begin considering yourself a wealthy person. You and your bank account may not change the day you start thinking and acting as such, but something is happening to your subconscious mind that will manifest in one way or another if you don't entertain negativity. Also, it is impossible to predict how long your stardom, wellness, or wealth will last, so do not stop giving your best but also relax and have fun.

THE ROAD TO WEALTH IS BUILT ON SELLING AND PROMOTING

Become a great promoter of your purpose and never give up. It will only work if you decide to not quit.

TO BE RICHER AND FREER, WANT LESS

I think it is a French proverb that states, "The man who needs nothing, receives everything." Also, as we talked about previously, always live below your means.

THEY WHO HAVE THE MOST ARE NOT THE HAPPIEST, BUT THEY WHO NEED THE LEAST

True happiness is not determined by material possession but by our mindset and ability to find fulfillment with what we have. Seek contentment in the present moment and free yourself from the never-ending cycle of striving for more. In fact, we are truly rich and happy whenever we get control of our time, and a big part of the reason is because the more time we have, the more we are dedicated to assisting

---

223 Coco Chanel, "Coco Chanel Quotes," BrainyQuote.com, https://www.brainyquote. com/quotes/coco_chanel_100040.

others. Winston Churchill used to claim, "We make a living by what we get, but we make a life by what we give."[224]

FULFILLMENT COMES FROM ALTRUISM

Set goals, think big, work tirelessly, learn continuously, and foster community to embark on a transformative journey toward fulfillment and impact. Most of the happiest people are not the ones who achieve the most, but those who spend more time in a state of flow. Find what activities make the time fly when you do them.

RICHEST LEGACY? JUST BE KIND TO EVERYONE

Kindness is long lasting for two reasons. First, you cannot become rich and help others without building good relationships. Second, the real measure of our wealth is how much we'd be worth if we lost it all.

"MORE THAN A FULL MOON SHINING BRIGHTLY ON A CLEAR NIGHT, I PREFER TO SEE A MOON THAT IS PARTIALLY HIDDEN BY CLOUDS"[225]

This quote is from Juko Murata, who is considered the creator of the tea ceremony. In Japan, the essence of beauty is very different, alluding to the imperfect, the details, the value of the passage of time and the wabi sabi, or asymmetry that creates unique pieces and people. Life, as shared here several times, is not fair nor easy and is constantly changing, but if we appreciate the beauty in its imperfection and impermanence, peacefully accept our natural cycle of growth (and decay), and look beyond, finding the hidden beauty of people, things,

---

224 Winston Churchill, "Winston Churchill Quotes," BrainyQuote.com, https://www. brainyquote.com/quotes/winston_churchill_131192.

225 "An Introduction to Chado," Urasenke Chado, https://www.urasenke.or.jp/texte/ about/chado/.

events, and being grateful for all these imperfections of life, we will be truly rich.

LEARN FROM THE JEWISH CULTURE

One interesting learning, from my philosophy and theology studies in London University, was the Jewish education from which many of their behaviors are derived when it comes to managing their finances. The Torah—which is what Christians know as the first five books of the Bible—and the Talmud—a book that gathers a series of rabbinical discussions that we could say are the open interpretation of the first one—are the basis of their financial success.

Knowledge is a fundamental pillar for us all, and Jewish culture greatly values it. Nearly all Jewish adults aged twenty-five and older (99 percent) have at least some primary education, and 61 percent have postsecondary degrees.[226]

Also, diversifying wealth is a must. Jewish teachings explain that a person should distribute wealth by the thirds rule: one part in land, another part in one's own business, and the last part in cash or investments. In fact, with just over nine million inhabitants, Israel alone has more companies listed on Nasdaq (sixty-plus companies) than all of Europe. Overall, more than 3,500 start-ups are listed, one for every 1,800 Israelis. Calvin Klein, Ralph Laurent, Michael Bloomberg, and Mark Zuckerberg, to name a brief sample, are Jewish.

Jewish culture teaches to live frugally below your economic possibilities and avoid bad debts. It is very difficult to see a Jew, no matter how prosperous he may be, squandering money on luxuries. For them it is better to have economic power than to show it to others. Money should always be a means and not the end. To define this, Jews use the

---

226 "Jewish Educational Attainment," Pew Research Center, December 13, 2016, https://www.pewresearch.org/religion/2016/12/13/jewish-educational-attainment.

word "Kesef." So, try out a more frugal style of living and consuming. You may find you need less than you think to be happy.

Finally, Jewish culture also teaches to be humble, honest with others, to maintain a good reputation when doing business, and the importance of giving generously. I have always liked the Yiddish concept of "Mensch," who is a person of high integrity and honor and something we should practice, Jews and non-Jews, much more often.

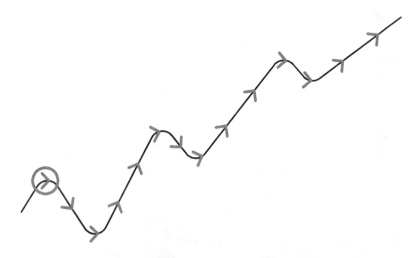

Remember that your life doesn't have to be a straight line of successes and advancements. The road may be filled with ups and downs, and that can lead to progress. As Graham Weaver, the founder of Alpine Investors, shares, "In life, sometimes, to keep going up, you have to go down," and he adds "Do your thing. Do it for decades. Write your story."

I hope the words and lessons from the chapters in this book can be put into practice. For me, it has been a process to collect my preferred quotes, thoughts, and organize them. After all, I never thought I would write a book, let alone one in English.

Though the work began with that wonderful present from my daughters of a jar full of "Dad life lessons" (as in the movies based on real events, I share with you a picture of the original jar here at the end), it has expanded into additional lessons on life, business, and investing and I hope that you, dear reader, can apply some of them to your life.

I'd like to add a message to readers who are parents: If you have adult children who receive regular financial support, they will be more interested in spending than saving. It's impossible to sustain family wealth for generations if you don't explain how to be good at the money game to your children. Our goal as parents should be to grow our children into independent adults with the capacity to save a fraction of what they earn—ideally, no less than 10 percent of their paycheck, whatever the amount—and to invest it in a smart way.

By the way, get in touch with me if you know of somebody who would be genuinely interested in this book but lacks the funds to buy one. I will gladly email them a copy in digital format.

Finally, I would like to share that I did not write this book to be read but to be proactively listened to. By that, I mean I am hoping that some of these pieces of advice, thoughts, and quotes motivate and inspire you to act.

If so, I would love to hear about your proactivity and results, along with the lessons you learned.

Be smarter, be a force for good, and above all, be kind. See you soon ;)

You can contact me at https://www.linkedin.com/in/fors.

Miami, March 24, 2024

RECOMMENDED READING

Here are some books on investing to get you started:

- *The Intelligent Investor* by Ben Graham. Known as the father of value investing and a key mentor for Warren Buffett, Graham shares his learnings in this book. Buffett has called this book, "by far the best book on investing ever written."[227]
- *Common Stocks and Uncommon Profits* by Philip Fisher. Warren Buffett says that his own investing approach is a combination of Ben Graham's and Fisher's—it's hard to receive higher praise than that![228]

---

227 "Warren Buffett—the Best Book on Investing and What It Can Teach You," FS Blog, https://fs.blog/warren-buffett-the-best-book-on-investing-and-what-it-can-teach-you/.

228 Gertie Fourie, "Warren Buffett's Investment Style: 85% Benjamin Graham and 15% Phil Fisher," BizNews.com, September 30, 2022, https://www.biznews.com/wealth-advisors/2022/09/30/warren-buffett-investment-style.

- *Beating the Street* by Peter Lynch. As the longtime fund manager for Fidelity's Magellan fund, Lynch is one of the most highly regarded investors on the planet.
- *The Little Book That Still Beats the Market* by Joel Greenblatt. In this one, you will learn a "magic formula" for investing. It consists of looking at earnings yield (EBIT/Enterprise Value) and return on capital (EBIT/(Net Working Capital + Net Fixed Assets)) to evaluate stocks. You'll see how to rank and combine these two factors to find winning companies.
- *The Essays of Warren Buffett* by Warren Buffett and Lawrence Cunningham. You'll find annual letters to Berkshire Hathaway shareholders, and they cover a wide range of topics. You'll learn everything from investing strategies to corporate governance.
- *The Outsiders* by William Thorndike. In this book, Thorndike narrates the stories of eight unconventional CEOs who went against the grain and created outstanding returns for their shareholders. It is one of the best books you'll find on how to think differently and get rewarded for it.
- *Rule #1* by Phil Town. Through this book, I learned how to find wide-moat companies, that is, those that have some kind of monopolistic position in the market, because of their "wide moats." These includes brands (McDonald's, Coke, Pepsi), patents (Pfizer, Intel, IBM), toll collections (media companies, agencies, utilities), hard switching companies (Apple, Microsoft, Harley), and/or price differentiators (Walmart, Costco, Target). You will learn what KPIs to analyze and how to compare them with their industry averages. You will understand the basics of ROIC (return on invested capital), sales growth rate, EPS (earnings per share) growth, BVPS (book per

value share), and FCF (free cash flow), and how to calculate the buying and selling price.

- *The Man Who Solved the Market: How Jim Simons Launched the Quant Revolution* by Jim Simons. This book is a biography that delves into the life and achievements of Jim Simons, a mathematician and hedge fund manager who revolutionized the field of finance through quantitative trading strategies. Offers unique insights into Simons's secretive hedge fund, Renaissance Technologies, and its unprecedented success using mathematical models and data analysis to outperform traditional investment strategies.

ABOUT THE AUTHOR

Fernando Ors Villajero (born May 19, 1969) is a European-born American economist, strategy consultant, digital intrapreneur and entrepreneur, venture capitalist, alternative investments expert, and author.

He is currently chairman of Reental, a leading global tokenization investing firm; CEO of Savia Group (Savia Consulting, Savia Health, Savia Capital, and Nueva Savia); CGO of Protein Capital, a venture capital fund pioneering excellence in digital asset, blockchain, web3, and AI companies investing; General Partner of Virtuous Capital, a multigenerational homes syndicated investment fund; General Partner of Fidelitas ARTe, the first art fintech company with a financial value-added and comprehensive personalized management for artists and art investors; and Board Member of Nash21, the first insurtech platform tokenizing and trading smart rental contracts, and Orbyn, the first fintech for alternative financial products and services tailored for both companies and investors.

He holds a double degree in business administration and economics, an MBA from IESE, and a master's in finance from CEF.

He has also participated in programs at Harvard Business School, Stanford, MIT, and Berkeley.

A transformational leader in high-growth and digital businesses, Ors has enjoyed several startup launches, exits, and IPOs, among others, Codere Interactiva (currently NASDAQ: CDRO), and Codere Group (BME: CDRE) with a ten-fold increase in revenues and profits before its unicorn valuation IPO (6xEBITDA price, $1.3 billion) during his tenure.

Ors's other previous executive positions include CEO of Bright-Star Coral Gables, global vice president of the Canadian consulting and SaaS firm FreeBalance, and president of the technology company Intralot in the United States.

Also known as FORS (an acronym that reminds him of Focus On Relationships and Service, and being a *fors* for good), he is driven to look for ways to make a positive impact on people's lives and the world around us, which he uses as a theme in all of his business ventures.

Ors has lived and worked in more than ten countries in Asia, Europe, and North America. He has traveled extensively and managed international teams of more than twenty nationalities. Ors is fluent in Spanish and English, has a working knowledge of French and Italian, and a basic understanding of Indonesian.

In his free time, Ors enjoys a variety of hobbies, including swimming in the ocean, forest bathing, reading inspirational books, watching movies based on real events, and playing the clarinet and saxophone. He practices Zen meditation, Krav Maga, and holds a Sandan black belt in Karate, for which he is known in the dojo as Sensei Fors. He lives with his wife and two daughters, as he always wanted to, on an island in Miami.

www.ingramcontent.com/pod-product-compliance
Lightning Source LLC
LaVergne TN
LVHW041203050326
832903LV00020B/430